Teach Me Your Ways

KAY ARTHUR

HARVEST HOUSE™ PUBLISHERS

EUGENE, OREGON

Cover by Koechel Peterson & Associates, Inc., Minneapolis, Minnesota

The New Inductive Study Series
TEACH ME YOUR WAYS
Copyright © 1994 by Precept Ministries International
Published by Harvest House Publishers
Eugene, Oregon 97402

Library of Congress Cataloging-in-Publication Data

Arthur, Kay, 1933-
        Teach me your ways / Kay Arthur.
            p. cm. — (The new inductive study series)
        ISBN 0-7369-0805-6
        1. Bible. O.T. Pentateuch—Criticism, interpretation, etc. 2. Bible. O.T. Pentateuch—Study and teaching. I. Title. II. Series: Arthur, Kay, 1933- The new inductive study series.
BS1225.2.A77   1994
222'.1'007—dc20

                                                                93-33925
                                                                CIP

Printed in the United States of America.

05 06 07 08 09 10 / BP / 10 9 8 7 6 5 4

CONTENTS

︾︾︾︾

How to Get Started...

Sometimes it's hard to read directions. You simply want to get started, and only if all else fails will you read the directions. I understand, but in this case, don't do it! These instructions are part of getting started, and they will help you greatly.

FIRST

As you study the books of the Pentateuch you will need four things in addition to this book:

1. A Bible that you are willing to mark in. The marking is essential. An ideal Bible for this purpose is *The New Inductive Study Bible (NISB)*. The *NISB* is in a single-column text format with larger, easy-to-read type, which is ideal for marking. The margins around the text are wide for note-taking.

The *NISB* also has instructions for studying each book of the Bible, but it does not contain any commentary on the text, nor is it compiled from any theological stance. Its purpose is to teach you how to discern truth for yourself through the inductive method of study. (The various charts and maps that you will find in this study guide are taken from the *NISB*.)

Whatever Bible you use, just know you will need to mark in it, which brings me to the second item you will need . . .

2. A fine-point, four-color ballpoint pen or various colored fine-point pens that you can use to write in your Bible. The Micron pens are best for this purpose. Office supply stores should have these.

3. Colored pencils or an eight-color Pentel pencil.

4. A composition book or loose-leaf notebook for working on your assignments and recording your insights.

SECOND

Though you will be given specific instructions for each day's study, there are basic things you need to know, do, and/or remember as you move through each book chapter by chapter.

1. As you read each chapter, train yourself to ask the "5 W's and an H": who, what, when, where, why, and how. Asking questions like these will help you see exactly what the Word of God has to say. When you interrogate the text with the 5 W's and an H, you would ask questions like this:

   a. **What** is this chapter about?
   b. **Who** are the main characters?
   c. **When** does this event or teaching take place?
   d. **Where** does this happen?
   e. **Why** is this being done or said?
   f. **How** did it happen?

2. The "when" of events or teachings is very important and should be marked in an easily recognizable way in your Bible. I do this by putting a clock in the margin of my *NISB*. You may want to underline or color the references to time in one specific color.

Remember, time may be expressed in several different ways: by mentioning an actual year, month, day, or by mentioning an event such as a feast, a year of a person's reign, etc. Time can also be indicated by words such as *then, when, afterwards, at this time,* etc.

3. There are certain key words you will want to mark in a special way in the text of your Bible. This is the purpose of the colored pencils and the colored pen. Developing the habit of marking your Bible in this way will make a significant difference in the way you study and in how much you remember.

A **key word** is an important word that is used by the author repeatedly in order to convey his message to his reader. There are certain key words or phrases that will show up throughout the book as a whole, while others will be concentrated in certain chapters or segments of the book. When you mark a key word, also mark its pronouns (*he, his, she, her, it, we, they, us, our, you, them, their*) and its synonyms.

For instance, one of the key words you will mark in Genesis is *covenant.* I color the word *covenant* the same way throughout my *NISB.* I color it red and box it in yellow.

You need to devise a color-coding system for these words so that when you look at a page of your Bible, you will instantly see where a particular word is used. When you start marking key words in various colors and symbols, it is easy to forget how you are marking certain words. Therefore, you may wish to use the bottom portion of the perforated card in the back of this book to write your key words on. Mark the words the way you plan to mark them in your Bible and then use the card as a bookmark.

Marking words for easy identification can be done by colors, symbols, or a combination of colors and symbols. However, colors are easier to distinguish than symbols. If I use symbols, I keep them very simple. For example, I color *repent* yellow but put a red arrow ↶ over it also. The symbol conveys the meaning of repent: a change of mind.

When I mark the members of the Godhead (which I do not always mark), I color every reference to the Father, Son, or Holy Spirit in yellow. I also use a purple pen and mark the Father with a triangle △ , symbolizing the Trinity. I mark the Son this way ⟋⟍ , and the Holy Spirit this way ⟋⟋⟋⟋ .

4. Because locations are important in a historical or biographical book of the Bible, you will find it helpful to mark these in a distinguishable way. I simply underline every reference to location in green (grass and trees are green!), using my four-color ballpoint pen.

I also look up the locations on maps so I can put myself into context geographically. If you have an *NISB* you will find maps right in the text.

5. When you finish studying a chapter, record the main theme of that chapter on the AT A GLANCE chart (located at the end of each book's study). Record it on the line beside the appropriate chapter number. If you have an *NISB*, you will want to record the chapter themes on the AT A GLANCE Chart at the end of each book in your Bible. Then you will have a permanent record of your studies right in your Bible, which will be helpful for future reference.

6. If you are doing this study within the framework of a class and you find the lessons too heavy, then simply do what you can. To do a little is better than to do nothing. Don't be an all-or-nothing person when it comes to Bible study.

Remember, anytime you get into the Word of God, you enter into more intensive warfare with the devil (our enemy). Why? Every piece of the Christian's armor is related to the Word of God. And our one and only offensive weapon is the sword of the Spirit, which is the Word of

God. The devil wants you to have a dull sword. Don't cooperate! You don't have to!

7. Every day when you finish your lesson, meditate on what you saw and ask your heavenly Father how you should live in the light of the truths you have just seen. At times, depending on how God has spoken to you, you might even want to record these "Lessons for Life" in the margin of your Bible next to the text you studied. The *NISB* suggests you simply put "LFL" in the margin of your Bible and then as briefly as possible record the lessons for life you want to remember.

8. Always begin your studies with prayer. As you do your part to handle the Word of God accurately, you must remember that the Bible is a divinely inspired book. The words that you are reading are truth, given to you by God that you might know Him and His ways. These truths are divinely revealed.

> For to us God revealed them through the Spirit; for the Spirit searches all things, even the depths of God. For who among men knows the thoughts of a man except the spirit of the man which is in him? Even so the thoughts of God no one knows except the Spirit of God (1 Corinthians 2:10,11).

Therefore, ask God to reveal His truth to you, to lead you and guide you into all truth. He will, if you will ask.

THIRD

This study book is designed to put you into the Word of God on a *daily* basis. Since man does not live by bread alone but by every word that comes out of the mouth of God, we each need a daily helping.

The assignments cover seven days; however, the seventh day is different from the other days. On the seventh day, the focus is on a major truth covered in that week's study.

You will find a verse or two to memorize and STORE IN YOUR HEART. Then there is a passage to READ AND DISCUSS. This will be extremely profitable for those who are using this material in a class setting, for it will cause the class to focus their attention on a critical portion of Scripture. To aid the individual and/or the class, there's a set of QUESTIONS FOR DISCUSSION OR INDIVIDUAL STUDY. This is followed with a THOUGHT FOR THE WEEK which will help you understand how to walk in the light of what you learned.

When you discuss the week's lesson, be sure to support your answers and insights from the Bible itself. Then you will be handling the Word of God in a way that will find His approval. Always examine your insights by carefully observing the text to see what it *says*. Then, before you decide what a Scripture or passage *means*, make sure you interpret it in the light of its context.

Scripture will never contradict Scripture. If it ever seems to, you can be certain that somewhere something is being taken out of context. If you come to a passage that is difficult to deal with, reserve your interpretations for a time when you can study the passage in greater depth.

Books in The New Inductive Study Series are survey courses. If you want to do a more in-depth study of a particular book of the Bible, we would suggest you do a Precept Upon Precept Bible Study Course on that book. You may obtain more information on these studies by contacting Precept Ministries at 800-763-8280, visiting our website at www.precept.org, or by filling out and mailing the response card at the back of this book.

GENESIS

GENESIS
AND ALL THINGS WERE
CREATED BY HIM AND FOR HIM...

∾∾∾∾

Genesis is the book of beginnings. If you want to know where it all started—creation, man, marriage, sin, civilizations, etc., then Genesis is the book you want to study. Genesis lays the foundation for the entire Word of God.

As you read through Genesis, you will find that the first 11 chapters cover four major events: creation, the fall of man, the flood, and the creation of the nations through the confusion of the languages at the tower of Babel.

The rest of Genesis, chapters 12 through 50, will center around four major characters: Abraham, Isaac, Jacob (Israel), and Joseph.

In eight short weeks you will not only have a good grasp of this critical book, but you will find yourself coming to a more intimate knowledge of your God and His ways. And to know and respond to such insight is to be transformed!

WEEK ONE

DAY ONE

Read Genesis 1. In distinctive ways or colors mark each occurrence of the following two phrases: *Then God said* and *There was evening and there was morning, (a)*_____ *day.*

Note what was created, how it was created, and when it was created. If there is room, record this in the margin of your Bible next to the appropriate verses.

As you finish reading each chapter of Genesis, record the theme of that chapter on the GENESIS AT A GLANCE chart (pages 44-45). The theme of a chapter is discerned by observing the subject or the person which is dealt with the most in that chapter. You may also want to record the theme in your Bible by the chapter number.

DAY TWO

As you study the Bible you will see that sometimes the author explains something and then comes back to the same subject and covers it again, this time giving additional insight to what was said in the first incident.

Carefully read Genesis 2, as it gives a more detailed account of what God did when He created the heavens and the earth.

As you read, carefully list God's instructions to the man. Also note how woman was created and what the relationship of man and woman was to be like.

List your insights in your notebook. If you have room in the margin of your Bible, you may want to record your insights there. Do this throughout this course. If you record your notes in your Bible, you will always have them with you.

Read Matthew 19:3-9, as it is an excellent cross-reference. Note how it relates to Genesis 2; then, if you want to remember this passage in relationship to Genesis, put the "address" of the verses in Matthew next to the Scripture it relates to in Genesis 2.

DAY THREE

Read Genesis 3 and Revelation 12:9; 20:2. Mark every reference to the serpent (Satan, devil, etc.) with a red pitchfork. List all you learn about him and his tactics.

DAY FOUR

Read Genesis 3 again. This time concentrate on the woman. Ask the 5 W's and an H: who, what, when, where, why, and how about the woman and what she does in this chapter.

List all you learn about the woman, including what she is named and why.

Note the progression of her actions that lead up to eating the fruit of the tree of the knowledge of good and evil.

List what God says will happen to the serpent, Adam, and the woman.

DAY FIVE

Read Genesis 4. List what you learn about Cain and about Abel. Then trace Cain's offspring in this chapter. Note what these men did. It will give you insight into the earliest civilization of man.

DAY SIX

Read Genesis 4:25–5:32. Watch what you learn about Seth and Enosh. Mark the word *likeness* and note the contrast between the two occurrences of this word. Also mark the key repeated phrase *and he died* and note in the margin of your Bible how long each man lived before he died.

Study the chart on page 46 and note that Adam is a contemporary of Lamech, Lamech of Noah, Noah of Abraham. Interesting, isn't it!

DAY SEVEN

Store in your heart: Genesis 3:15.

Read and discuss: Genesis 3:1-15; Romans 5:12; 3:10-12; Isaiah 53:6.

QUESTIONS FOR DISCUSSION OR INDIVIDUAL STUDY

- What do you learn from these verses about sin? For instance, from what Adam and Eve did, and from the way the serpent tempted Eve, what would you say sin is? List your insights and discuss them.

- Maybe you know some other verses that define sin. If so, share them.

∾ What do you learn from Genesis and the other verses about the consequences of sin?

∾ If the root of sin is "turning your own way"—i.e., walking independently of God—what would the fruit of such a lifestyle be?

∾ Who or what would you say governs your life? How do you know? Why?

∾ Genesis is the book of beginnings. If there is time, discuss the "firsts" you have seen in these five chapters of Genesis (first man and woman, etc.).

∾ How do the truths of Genesis 1–5 compare with things you have been taught by others? Who are you going to believe?

THOUGHT FOR THE WEEK

Have you recognized that you are a sinner and that there is only One who can grant you forgiveness of sins and set you free from slavery to sin? It is the Lord Jesus Christ, the seed of the woman who bruised the serpent's head.

> Now the birth of Jesus Christ was as follows: When His mother Mary had been betrothed to Joseph, before they came together she was found to be with child by the Holy Spirit. And Joseph her husband, being a righteous man and not wanting to disgrace her, planned to send her away secretly. But when he had considered this, behold, an angel of the Lord appeared to him in a dream, saying, "Joseph, son of David, do not be afraid to take Mary as your wife; for the child who has been conceived in her is of the Holy Spirit. And she will bear a Son; and you shall call His name Jesus, for He will save His people from their sins" (Matthew 1:18-21).

WEEK TWO

DAY ONE

Read Genesis 6. Mark every reference to *man*. Include the appropriate pronouns; however, do not mark "sons of God." List what you learn from your markings.

Also mark the word *covenant*, then list in the margin of your Bible what you learn about the covenant. Also mark every reference to Noah and list what you learn about him.

DAY TWO

Read Genesis 7. Mark every reference to time. You may want to draw a little clock in the margin so that your eye is drawn to the time phrases. Also mark every reference to Noah and to the ark. Make a list of all you learn regarding the ark.

DAY THREE

Read Genesis 8. Mark every reference to time and to Noah. List what you learn regarding Noah.

DAY FOUR

Read Genesis 9. Mark every occurrence of the word *covenant.* Also mark every reference to Noah. List what you learn from marking *covenant* and the references to Noah.

Compare Genesis 9:5,6 with Numbers 35:29-34 and Deuteronomy 21:1-9.

DAY FIVE

Read Genesis 10. Note the sons of Japheth, Ham, and Shem. Watch the repetition of the phrase *according to* and see what you observe. You will find it interesting to study the map on page 20.

Note what happens in Genesis 10:25.

DAY SIX

Read Genesis 11. Mark the word *language* and list all you learn from marking this word. Also mark the word *Babel* in this chapter and in Genesis 10:10. List what you learn about Babel in your notebook. (If you have a *NISB,* use the chart on page 2074 to compile your insights.)

DAY SEVEN

Store in your heart: Genesis 6:7,8.

Read and discuss: Genesis 6; 7:11-23; 2 Peter 3:3-7; Matthew 24:36-44. Discuss all you learn about the flood by asking the 5 W's and an H and then letting your answers come from these Scriptures. Make sure you cover the reason for the flood.

QUESTIONS FOR DISCUSSION OR INDIVIDUAL STUDY

∾ According to 2 Peter 3:3-7, do all people accept the fact of a universal flood? Why do you think they respond the way they do?

∾ In Matthew 24:36-44, Jesus uses the flood for an illustration. What was the point He was making regarding the flood when He compared it to the second coming of our Lord Jesus Christ?

∾ People are quick to believe that God is a God of love, yet they have a hard time accepting the fact that God judges. Why do you think this is?

∾ How do you feel when you hear of the judgment of God?

∾ What have you learned this week about God and His ways?

THOUGHT FOR THE WEEK

The days just before the coming of the Son of Man, the Lord Jesus Christ, are likened to the days of Noah. Those who do not believe in the second coming of our Lord and the judgment connected with that event will not be prepared for it any more than the people were in Noah's day. How are you living? Are you on the alert, aware that the Lord could come at any time? Are you prepared to meet your God face-to-face?

THE SETTLEMENT OF THE DESCENDANTS OF SHEM, HAM, AND JAPHETH

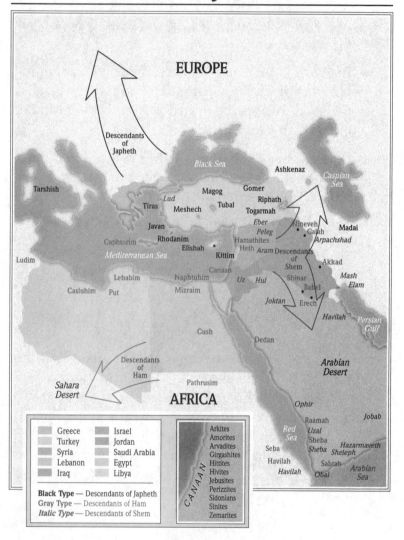

EUROPE

Descendants of Japheth

Black Sea

Ashkenaz

Caspian Sea

Tarshish

Magog Gomer
Lud Riphath
Tiras Meshech Tubal Togarmah

Eber
Peleg Nineveh
Calah Madai
Arpachshad

Javan

Caphtorim Rhodanim Hamathites
Elishah Heth Aram Descendants of Shem

Kittim

Akkad

Ludim Mediterranean Sea

Canaan

Lehabim Naphtuhim Uz Hul Shinar Mash
Casluhim Put Mizraim Babel Elam
Joktan Erech

Havilah Persian Gulf

Cush

Descendants of Ham

Dedan

Arabian Desert

Sahara Desert Pathrusim

AFRICA

Ophir

Raamah Jobab
Red Sea Uzal Sheba
Seba Sheba Sheleph Hazarmaveth
Havilah Sabtah
Havilah Obal Arabian Sea

Greece	Israel
Turkey	Jordan
Syria	Saudi Arabia
Lebanon	Egypt
Iraq	Libya

Arkites
Amorites
Arvadites
Girgashites
Hittites
Hivites
Jebusites
Perizzites
Sidonians
Sinites
Zemarites

CANAAN

Black Type — Descendants of Japheth
Gray Type — Descendants of Ham
Italic Type — Descendants of Shem

WEEK THREE

ตนตนตนตน

DAY ONE

Read Genesis 11:26–12:20. Mark every reference to Abram and list everything you learn about him from this passage of Scripture. When you discover how old Abram is, note it in the margin of your Bible. (Later on you will read where Abram's name is changed by God to Abraham.)

As you read today's lesson, consult the map below.

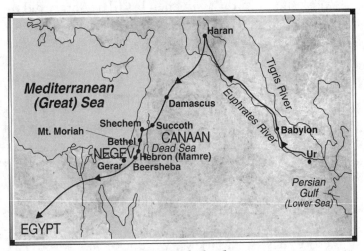

Journeys of Abraham

DAY TWO

Read Genesis 13. Mark every reference to Abram, Lot, and Sodom. Note what God says to Abram, when He says it, and Abram's response to it.

DAY THREE

Read Genesis 14. Mark every reference to Abram, Lot, Sodom and Gomorrah, and Melchizedek. Make a list of what you learn about each.

If you have time, read Hebrews 6:19–7:6.

DAY FOUR

Read Genesis 15. Summarize and list God's promises to Abram.

Mark the word *covenant*, then list what Abram did on that day, what happened, what God promised, and what God told Abram would come to pass.

DAY FIVE

Read Genesis 16. There are four main characters in this chapter. List what you learn about Sarai, Abram, Hagar, and Ishmael. Note Abram's age in the margin of your Bible.

DAY SIX

Read Genesis 17. Mark the word *covenant* as you have done previously. Also mark in another distinctive way the word *circumcised*. List what you learn about Abram, Sarai, Ishmael, and Isaac. Leave room to add to your list as you gain more information moving through the book of Genesis.

Note Abraham's age in the margin.

DAY SEVEN

Store in your heart: Genesis 15:6.

Read and discuss: Genesis 12:1-3; 15:1-21; Galatians 3:6-9. If you have adequate time you may also want to discuss Romans 4:1-12,16-22.

QUESTIONS FOR DISCUSSION OR INDIVIDUAL STUDY

∾ What exactly did God promise Abram in Genesis 12:1-3?

∾ Discuss the way in which God dealt with Abram in Genesis 15. What exactly did God do when He made a covenant with Abraham? The Hebrew word for covenant means a compact or agreement made by passing through pieces of flesh.

∾ What were the conditions of the covenant? On whose part?

∾ How old would Abraham and Sarah have been when Isaac was born?

∾ As you think about God's dealings with Abraham, what do you learn about God and His ways? Does He keep His promises? Does He always move immediately to fulfill His Word? Why do you think God moves as He does?

ை What did you learn about God and about Abraham's faith that you can apply to your own life?

ை What did you learn about circumcision this week? What was the reason for circumcision? How important was it for a person to be circumcised?

THOUGHT FOR THE WEEK

What are you trusting in for your salvation—works, circumcision, baptism, or the promises of God? On what basis was Abraham, who was born a sinner, declared righteous before God? Are you any greater than Abraham, or any less a sinner?

> For by grace you have been saved through faith; and that not of yourselves, it is the gift of God; not as a result of works, that no one may boast. For we are His workmanship, created in Christ Jesus for good works, which God prepared beforehand so that we would walk in them (Ephesians 2:8-10).

WEEK FOUR

DAY ONE

Read Genesis 18. Note God's promise to Sarah and her response. What do you learn from this chapter about the Lord's relationship to Abraham and the action the Lord is about to take in respect to Sodom and Gomorrah? Examine it in the light of the 5 W's and an H.

DAY TWO

Read Genesis 19. Follow the details of this account very carefully. List all you learn about the people of Sodom and Lot's relationship to them. Also note the response of the different members of Lot's family to Lot and to the situation.

If you have time, read 2 Peter 2:1-10a and note what you learn about Sodom and Gomorrah and about Lot.

DAY THREE

Read Genesis 20. Continue to make lists or add to existing lists what you learn about the three main people mentioned in this chapter: Abraham, Sarah, and Abimelech.

DAY FOUR

Read Genesis 21. Record what you learn regarding Abraham, Sarah, Isaac, Hagar, and Ishmael. Pay careful attention to the various relationships of these people in this chapter. Also mark the word *covenant* and record what you learn about Abraham and Abimelech.

Write the age of Abraham in the margin of your Bible. What age would Sarah be? Look at Genesis 17:17.

DAY FIVE

Read Genesis 22. Mark the following words: *love, worship,* and *obeyed.* Carefully note how they are used, for this is the first time these words are used in the book of Genesis. Also mark each occurrence of the word *lamb* and *ram* in the same way.

Also note what the name of the place was called and why.

DAY SIX

Read Genesis 23. Note what you learn about Abraham and Sarah.

DAY SEVEN

Store in your heart: Genesis 22:12.
Read and discuss: Genesis 21:1-12; 22:1-18; Hebrews 11:1,2,6,17-19.

QUESTIONS FOR DISCUSSION OR INDIVIDUAL STUDY

∾ What do you learn about the relationship between Isaac and Ishmael?

∾ Why would Abraham's descendants be named through Isaac rather than Ishmael, since Ishmael was born first?

∾ Why did God tell Abraham to offer Isaac as a burnt offering to Him? Why did Abraham obey God? How did Abraham feel about Isaac? How do you know?

∾ What do you learn about God and His ways from this passage?

∾ If you have time you may also want to discuss Genesis 19 and the issue of homosexuality, although this will be covered in the survey of Leviticus. If you discuss homosexuality, you will want to read Leviticus 18:22; 20:13; Romans 1:26,27; 1 Corinthians 6:9-11; Galatians 5:19-21; Jude 7; Revelation 21:7,8. You will want to discuss what you learn from each of these passages.

THOUGHT FOR THE WEEK

Is there something or someone you don't feel you can trust God with? When you hold everything and everyone in an open hand before God, when you are willing to put everything on the altar of obedience, God will know that you properly fear Him for who He is and what He has promised in His Word. Remember, He is "Jehovah (YHWH) Jireh," the Provider of all you will ever need.

> What then shall we say to these things? If God is for us, who is against us? He who did not spare His own Son, but delivered Him over for us all, how will He not also with Him freely give us all things? (Romans 8:31,32).

WEEK FIVE

DAY ONE

Read Genesis 24:1-28. Note carefully Abraham's instructions to his servant and the details of the events that follow.

DAY TWO

Read Genesis 24:29-49. Then review 24:1-49 and make a list of everything you learn about Rebekah from these verses. What kind of a woman is she?

DAY THREE

Read Genesis 24:50-67. Add to your list the things you learn about Rebekah from these verses. As you read 24:61-67 examine the meeting of Isaac and Rebekah in the light of the 5 W's and an H.

DAY FOUR

Read Genesis 25:1-20. Note the ages of Abraham and Isaac in the margin of your Bible next to the appropriate verses. List what you learn about Abraham, Isaac, and Ishmael from this chapter.

DAY FIVE

Read Genesis 25:19–26:35. List what you learn about Isaac, Jacob, and Esau. Also note any references to age in the margin of your Bible. Also mark any occurrence of the words *covenant* and *oath*.

DAY SIX

Read Genesis 27. Mark every occurrence of the word *bless* and its synonyms. Carefully observe the actions of Isaac, Rebekah, Jacob, and Esau. Also note the differences in their individual blessings.

DAY SEVEN

Store in your heart: Genesis 25:23,24 or Hebrews 12:15,16.

Read and discuss: Genesis 25:27-34; Hebrews 12:1-3, 14-17.

QUESTIONS FOR DISCUSSION OR INDIVIDUAL STUDY

ᴗ What have you learned about Jacob and Esau this week?

ᴗ What is the birthright? Look up Deuteronomy 21:15-17. Why was it important?

ᴗ How did Esau treat his birthright? What does this tell you about Esau?

∾ What is your "birthright" as a child of God? How do you treat it? Why?

THOUGHT FOR THE WEEK

Esau looked to the immediate needs of today instead of the promises of tomorrow, and in doing so he sold his birthright for a mess of pottage. Is there anything you are tempted to offer on the altar of expediency—something that goes against your birthright or obligations as a child of God? Don't lose heart, for in due time you will reap the harvest of righteousness if you do not faint.

> Therefore we do not lose heart, but though our outer man is decaying, yet our inner man is being renewed day by day. For momentary, light affliction is producing for us an eternal weight of glory far beyond all comparison, while we look not at the things which are seen, but at the things which are not seen; for the things which are seen are temporal, but the things which are not seen are eternal (2 Corinthians 4:16-18).

Week Six

DAY ONE

Read Genesis 28. Mark the word *blessed* and its synonyms. Note what Esau does and what Jacob does. Watch Jacob's commitment to the Lord.

DAY TWO

Read Genesis 29. Carefully note what happens in the relationships of the following: Laban, Jacob, Rachel, and Leah.

DAY THREE

Read Genesis 30. Observe the conflict between Rachel and Leah. Note who is born to whom. Then observe Jacob and Laban's relationship and how Jacob prospers.

DAY FOUR

Read Genesis 31. Mark the word *covenant* and note the various things which are done as a testimony of the covenant. Note the word *Mizpah* and what it means.

DAY FIVE

Read Genesis 32. Note how Jacob prepares to meet Esau. Then note what happens when God meets with Jacob. You might want to highlight the verse that tells of Jacob's name being changed, and also note it in the margin of your Bible for quick reference.

DAY SIX

Read Genesis 33. Note what happens when Jacob meets Esau, then when Jacob moves on and settles in the land he purchases.

DAY SEVEN

Store in your heart: Genesis 32:28.

Read and discuss: Genesis 28:1-4,10-22; 32:22-32; John 1:51; 2 Peter 1:2-4.

QUESTIONS FOR DISCUSSION OR INDIVIDUAL STUDY

∾ Review the lives of Jacob and Esau to this point.

∾ What were God's promises to Jacob? Why did God make these promises? How did Jacob respond?

∾ What do you learn about Jacob's ladder from these passages?

∾ Why did Jacob wrestle with "the man"? What did it cost him? Was it worth it?

∾ Have you ever cared about God's blessing on your life enough to "wrestle with the Lord"? Share it.

∾ What was Jacob's name changed to? By whom?

THOUGHT FOR THE WEEK

Jesus Christ is God's only "ladder to heaven," so to speak, and heaven is reached through Him alone (John 14:6). The promises of God in Him are "yea and amen," and through Him and Him alone you have everything that pertains to life and godliness (2 Peter 1:2-4). You are complete in Him (Colossians 2:10). Don't let go of God and His promises until He blesses you. Strive with God in prayer, strive with men in faith, and you will prevail.

> Ask, and it will be given to you; seek, and you will find; knock, and it will be opened to you. For everyone who asks receives, and he who seeks finds, and to him who knocks it will be opened. Or what man is there among you who, when his son asks him for a loaf, will give him a stone? Or if he asks for a fish, he will not give him a snake, will he? If you then, being evil, know how to give good gifts to your children, how much more will your Father who is in heaven give what is good to those who ask Him! (Matthew 7:7-11).

WEEK SEVEN

DAY ONE

Read Genesis 33:18–34:31. Consult the map on page 21 to get your geographical bearings. Study this incident in the light of the 5 W's and an H. Read Genesis 49:5-7.

DAY TWO

Read Genesis 35. This is a significant chapter. Watch all that is done by God. To discern the meaning of Bethel, look at the footnote, if your Bible has one, for 35:15. Carefully observe what happens to each of the main characters mentioned in this chapter. Read Genesis 49:3,4 in connection with Reuben.

DAY THREE

Read Genesis 36. List the main facts you observe regarding Esau from this chapter. Note the name of the people he fathers. Consult the maps on pages 35 and 36 to see where they settle.

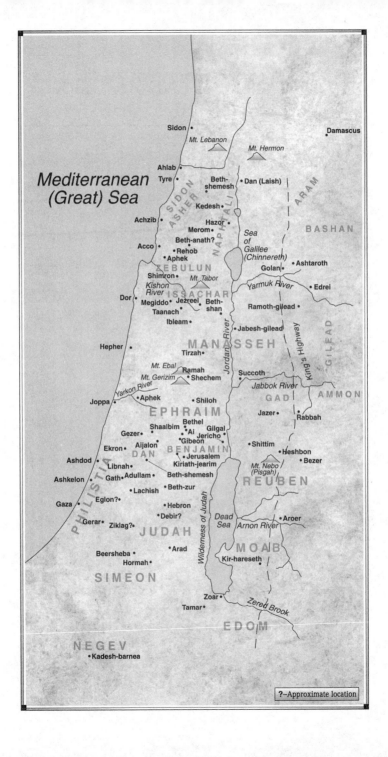

THE ANCIENT AND MODERN
SITES OF THE EXODUS

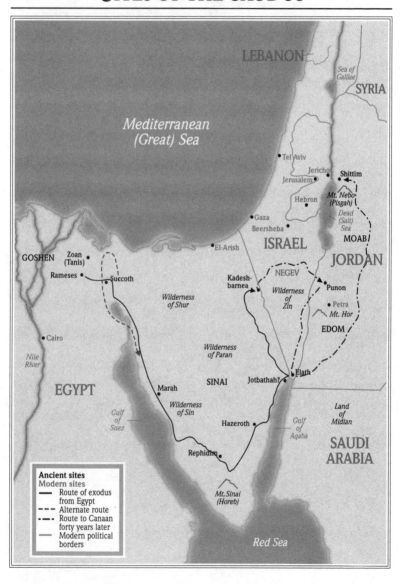

DAY FOUR

Read Genesis 37. List all you learn about Joseph. Also list the main points of Joseph's two dreams and watch how these dreams are interpreted by his brothers and by his father.

DAY FIVE

Read Genesis 38. Note all you learn regarding Judah and regarding Tamar. In the margin draw a simple diagram of Judah's offspring as described in this chapter, including through Tamar. Then read Matthew 1:1-3 and look for Perez on the chart of THE GENEALOGY OF JESUS THE CHRIST, page 39.

DAY SIX

Read Genesis 37:26-28,36; 39:1-23. Note how Judah behaved in respect to Joseph. List all you learn about Joseph from these verses. Pay careful attention to what the Lord did.

DAY SEVEN

Store in your heart: Genesis 39:9.

Read and discuss: Genesis 39:7-23; Proverbs 6:20-35; 7:1-27; Hebrews 13:4.

QUESTIONS FOR DISCUSSION OR INDIVIDUAL STUDY

∾ What did you learn about Joseph this week?

∽ What were "Mrs. Potiphar's" tactics, and how did Joseph handle them?

∽ What were the consequences of Joseph's actions? Do you think these consequences were warranted? How did Joseph handle what happened?

∽ What do you learn from Proverbs about "strange women" and the men who go after them? Discuss the man's ways, the woman's ways, and the consequences.

∽ What do you learn from Hebrews 13:4 about sex outside of marriage? What do you think would be some of the ways judgment would come? Do you think a person can violate this verse and get away with it? Why?

∽ What should you do when you are tempted "to lie" with someone you aren't married to?

THOUGHT FOR THE WEEK

When you are tempted to be immoral in thought, word, or deed, you need to remember Jesus' words of warning in Matthew 5:27-32.

Like Joseph, you need to "flee immorality" (1 Corinthians 6:18). "Everyone who looks at a woman" (Matthew 5:28) is in the present tense, which speaks not of a lustful thought that suddenly invades your mind but of allowing it to remain and continue there so that you "keep on looking." In the Greek language the present tense implies continuous or habitual action. You need to have the mind-set of Joseph: "How then could I do this great evil, and sin against God?" Do as Job did: "I have made a covenant with my eyes; how then could I gaze at a virgin?" (Job 31:1).

THE GENEALOGY OF JESUS THE CHRIST

As proof of His right to the throne of David through Mary

David

Adam (1 Chronicles 1–2 / Luke 3)
Seth
Enosh
Cainan
Mahalaleel
Lamech
NoahRam
Shem
Arphaxad
Cainan
Shelah
Heber
Peleg
Reu
Serug
Nahor
Terah
Abraham (1 Chronicles 3
Isaac (Matthew 1 / Luke 3)
Jacob
Judah
Perez
Hezron
Admin
Amminadab
Nahshon
Salmon—Rahab
Boaz—Ruth
Obed
Jesse

Nathan (Luke 3)
Mattatha
Menna
Melea
Eliakim
Jonam
Joseph
Judah
Simeon
Levi
Matthat
Jorim
Eliezer
Joshua
Er
Elmadam
Cosam
Addi
Melchi
Neri
Shealtiel
Zerubbabel
Rhesa
Joanan
Joda
Josech
Semein
Mattathias
Maath
Naggai
Hesli
Nahum
Amos
Mattathias
Joseph
Jannai
Melchi
Levi
Matthat
Eli
Mary

Solomon (1 Chronicles 3
Rehoboam (Matthew 1)
Abijah
Asa
Jehoshaphat
Joram (Jehoram)
Ahaziah
Joash
Amaziah
Uzziah (Azariah).
Jotham
Ahaz
Hezekiah
Manasseh
Amon
Josiah
Jehoiakim
Jeconiah (Jehoiachin)
Shealtiel
Zerubbabel (Matthew 1)
Abuid
Eliakim
Azor
Zadok
Achim
Eliud
Eleazar
Matthan
Jacob
Joseph

The Holy Spirit
Luke 1:35

Jesus
("Being supposedly the
son of Joseph"
[Luke 3:23])

WEEK EIGHT

~~~~~

DAY ONE

Read Genesis 40 and 41. Mark every occurrence of the word *dream*. In the margin of your Bible list each dream as well as the essence of the dream and its meaning. Note where proper interpretations of dreams come from. Also note any references to time.

DAY TWO

Read Genesis 37:5-8,18-24,29-35; 42:1-38. Observe what you learn about Reuben from these passages. Also carefully observe the response of Joseph and of the brothers to the events as they occur in Genesis 42.

DAY THREE

Read Genesis 43. Mark every reference to Benjamin. Then read Genesis 35:16-19,24. Consult the chart on page 41.

DAY FOUR

Read Genesis 44 and 45. Carefully observe Joseph's heart and behavior toward his brothers. See if you can find one verse which capsulizes why he responds the way he does.

DAY FIVE

Read Genesis 46 and 47. Note all that occurs in respect to Jacob (Israel) and to the brothers, including where they settle. Consult the map on page 35. Also note what God says to Jacob.

The Birth Order of Jacob's (Israel's) Sons	
Mother	**Son**
Leah	Reuben (born 1921 B.C.) Simeon Levi Judah
Bilhah (Rachel's maid)	Dan Naphtali
Zilpah (Leah's maid)	Gad Asher
Leah	Issachar Zebulun
Rachel	Joseph (born 1914 B.C.) Benjamin

DAY SIX

Read Genesis 48–50. Manasseh and Ephraim become important figures in relationship to the 12 tribes of Israel and their settlement in the promised land, so give careful attention to what you learn about them in these chapters. As you read Genesis 49 and Jacob's prophetic word regarding his sons, highlight the name of each of the sons so you can spot them easily.

DAY SEVEN

Store in your heart: Genesis 50:20.

Read and discuss: Genesis 50; 1Thessalonians 5:18; Isaiah 14:27; Romans 8:28-30.

QUESTIONS FOR DISCUSSION OR INDIVIDUAL STUDY

∾ What were the major events of Joseph's life that were covered in your study this week? List them and then discuss what you learn about Joseph from these events.

∾ How would you handle your brothers if they treated you the way Joseph was treated?

∾ Why did Joseph respond as he did? What can you learn from his response that you can apply to your own life? How can you apply it? What New Testament principles or Scriptures can help you and why?

THOUGHT FOR THE WEEK

No temptation [trial or testing] has overtaken you but such as is common to man; and God is faithful, who will not allow you to be tempted beyond what you are able, but with the temptation [trial or testing] will provide the way of escape also, that you will be able to endure it (1 Corinthians 10:13).

Through two dreams God prepared Joseph for the trials and temptations he would endure. Joseph would not permit a root of bitterness to spring up in his heart, to trouble him and defile others. Instead he believed God, clinging to Him in faith's obedience.

God even prepared Jacob and his sons, for in His sovereignty Joseph shared his dreams with them. Think what could have been Jacob's had he clung to the saying regarding Joseph's dream in Genesis 37:9-11!

Beloved, I don't know where you are or what you are going through, but I do know that because Genesis is a book of beginnings, this study could be a new beginning for you—the beginning of a life of faith, one where you determine that no matter what the circumstances you are going to cling in faith's obedience to the character of God and the veracity of His Word.

Remember, God has a purpose for your life. Whatever comes into your life cannot thwart that purpose, or God would not permit it. The close of your story has not yet been written. If you belong to God, if you love Him, whatever comes must result in your good and His glory (Romans 8:28). God will use your trials to "preserve many people alive" as they see your faith and desire to know your God the way you know Him.

GENESIS AT A GLANCE

Theme of Genesis:

SEGMENT DIVISIONS

Author: Moses (Luke 24:27)	THE FIRSTS	4 MAIN EVENTS/ 4 CHARACTERS	TIME SPANS		CHAPTER THEMES
Historical Setting:	MAN			1	
	MARRIAGE			2	
				3	
				4	
Purpose:		BEGINNINGS OF MAN	APPROXIMATELY 2080 YEARS	5	
				6	
				7	
Key Words: (include synonyms)				8	
				9	
				10	
				11	
				12	
				13	
				14	
		BEGINNINGS OF ISRAEL *(CONTINUED NEXT PAGE)*	APPROXIMATELY 300 YEARS *(CONTINUED NEXT PAGE)*	15	
				16	
				17	
				18	
				19	
				20	
				21	
				22	
				23	
				24	
				25	

SEGMENT DIVISIONS

THE FIRSTS		CHARACTERS 4	TIME SPANS	CHAPTER THEMES
		BEGINNINGS OF ISRAEL	APPROXIMATELY 300 YEARS	26
				27
				28
				29
				30
				31
				32
				33
				34
				35
				36
				37
				38
				39
				40
				41
				42
				43
				44
				45
				46
				47
				48
				49
				50

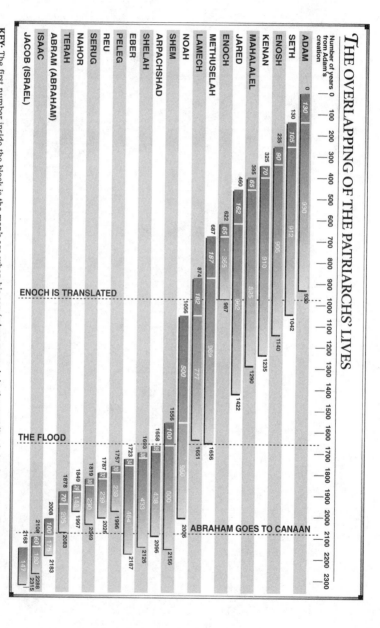

THE OVERLAPPING OF THE PATRIARCHS' LIVES

KEY: The first number inside the block is the man's age when his son (whose name is in the next line below) was born. The second number in the block is the number of years the man lived. The numbers preceding and following each block are the number of years from Adam's creation.

ENOCH IS TRANSLATED

THE FLOOD

ABRAHAM GOES TO CANAAN

EXODUS

EXODUS
I Am Everything and Anything You'll Ever Need...
꙳ ꙳ ꙳ ꙳ ꙳

On the day that God passed through the offering pieces in a flaming torch and a smoking oven when He made a covenant with Abraham, He told Abraham that he could know for certain that his "descendants will be strangers in a land that is not theirs, where they will be enslaved and oppressed four hundred years. But I will also judge the nation whom they will serve; and afterward they will come out with many possessions" (Genesis 15:13,14).

For 30 years the sons of Israel lived in Egypt under the favor and protection of Pharaoh. Then there arose a new Pharaoh who did not know Joseph, a Pharaoh who feared this people who had multiplied so greatly in his land. And so the sons of Israel became slaves in Egypt.

That slavery lasted 400 years. Then the Israelites cried out to their God, and the exodus began.

GENERAL INSTRUCTIONS

1. Use a five-by-seven card to make a long, narrow bookmark for your survey study of Exodus. On that card make a list of the key words that follow. Then code each key word, along with its synonyms and personal pronouns, in a distinctive way. You might want to color each word in a single color or combination of colors, or you might want to draw a simple symbol around the word. If that is not enough to make it distinctive, color it.

   For instance, you could color the word *covenant* red and then box it in with yellow. The word *cloud* could simply be noted this way: (CLOUD)

   MAJOR KEY WORDS:
   slave(s) (bondage)
   deliver (delivered)
   holy
   the Lord commanded (I commanded)
   cloud
   tested
   law
   tabernacle (tent, tent of meeting)

2. As you complete your study of a chapter of Exodus, record the theme of that chapter on the EXODUS AT A

GLANCE chart (pages 82-83). This way you will always have a record of the content of Exodus, which you can consult at any time. You may also want to record the theme by the chapter number in your Bible.

3. If you have an *NISB*, you might also want to read through the THINGS TO DO and THINGS TO THINK ABOUT sections at the beginning of Exodus.

WEEK ONE

DAY ONE

Read Acts 7:1-20, as it will give you a synopsis of Israel's history up to the time of Exodus.

DAY TWO

Read Genesis 50:22-26 and Exodus 1. Note how Exodus relates to Genesis chronologically. Pharaoh is the title for the king of Egypt. List everything you learn about Pharaoh from this chapter.

DAY THREE

Read Exodus 2. List the main events in Moses' life as covered in this chapter. Also note what you learn about God.

DAY FOUR

Read Exodus 3. List all you learn about Moses from this chapter.

DAY FIVE

Read Acts 7:20-36 and list what you learn regarding Moses that you didn't see thus far in Exodus.

DAY SIX

Read Exodus 3 again. This time list everything you learn about God from this chapter, and everything you learn about His name. See John 8:23,24,56-59; 10:31-33.

As you read the verses in the Gospel of John, watch for and mark the phrase *I am*. If you see the word *He* in italics, it was added by the translator, so treat it as if it weren't in the text. Then list what you learn from marking *I am*.

DAY SEVEN

Store in your heart: Exodus 3:14; John 8:24.

Read and discuss: Exodus 3:13-15; John 8:23,24,56-59; 10:31-33. Discuss what you learn about Jesus Christ from these verses in John and the significance of their relationship to Exodus 3:13-15. Also discuss what you have learned about God—His character and His ways.

QUESTIONS FOR DISCUSSION OR INDIVIDUAL STUDY

∾ What did you learn about the Israelites, Moses, and God from your study of the first three chapters of Exodus? (If you are leading a class and have a white-board, you might want to make three columns and then list the insights of the class.)

ᑫ What specifically did you learn about the order of events in Moses' life as you integrated the insights from Acts 7 with the first three chapters of Exodus?

ᑫ What is God's memorial name? How long will that name be His? What does that name tell you about Him?

ᑫ What do you learn about the Lord Jesus Christ from comparing Exodus 3 with the passages you looked up in the Gospel of John? And what if you don't believe these truths? According to Jesus, are there any consequences to a person's unbelief?

THOUGHT FOR THE WEEK

Can you see the significance of studying the Old Testament as well as the New? One complements, supplements, or helps explain the other. Scripture interprets Scripture. This is why the apostle Paul was careful to teach the whole counsel of God and why you must devote yourself to knowing and understanding the entire Word of God.

When you combine Exodus 3:14 with John 8:24, it becomes clear that if you do not believe that Jesus Christ is God, then you will die in your sins. Beloved, where do you stand in relationship to God?

John stated his purpose in writing his Gospel in John 20:30,31:

> Therefore many other signs Jesus also performed in the presence of the disciples, which are not written in this book; but these have been written that you may believe that Jesus is the Christ, the

Son of God; and that believing you may have life
in His name.

Even as the Israelites were slaves to Pharaoh, so we are
born slaves to sin. Only God could deliver the children of
Israel out of bondage, out of the land of Egypt. Only Jesus
Christ can deliver you from the prince of this world, from
slavery to sin. Apart from acknowledging that Jesus Christ
is God and believing on Him as the one and only Savior,
there is no eternal life—only eternal death. How critical it
is that we understand and in faith embrace this truth and
then share it when we share the gospel of Jesus Christ.

WEEK TWO

As you read this week, mark the key words listed on your bookmark. Also note what you learn about God from these chapters. Remember, God's character never alters. He is the same yesterday, today, and forever. Observe Moses' relationship with God, then see what you can learn and apply to your own relationship with God.

Designate a couple of pages of your notebook for a running list of lessons that you learn from the life of Moses. As you observe Moses, watch what lessons on leadership you can glean from his life and record these.

DAY ONE

Read Exodus 4:1-17.

DAY TWO

Read Exodus 4:18-31. Compare Exodus 4:24-26 with Genesis 17:9-14.

DAY THREE

Read Exodus 5:1-14. Note Pharaoh's response to what God told Moses he was to do.

DAY FOUR

Read Exodus 5:15–6:1.

DAY FIVE

Read Exodus 6:1-9. Observe what God says regarding His name. God Almighty is *El Shaddai* in Hebrew. If you use a New American Standard Bible, whenever you see LORD in all capitals, you can know (unless otherwise noted) that it is the translation of YHWH. YHWH was the special name of God, which some scholars transliterate as Yahweh. It was a name not pronounced by the Jews because of its sacredness.

DAY SIX

Read Exodus 6:10–7:7. Watch again Moses' concern regarding his lack of skill in speech.

DAY SEVEN

Store in your heart: Exodus 4:11,12.
Read and discuss: Exodus 4:10-17; 6:10-13; 6:28–7:6; John 12:49; Matthew 10:19,20.

QUESTIONS FOR DISCUSSION OR INDIVIDUAL STUDY

∾ How did Moses feel about his calling from God? What was Moses apprehensive about, and what was Moses' solution to the situation?

∽ What does this tell you about Moses? Can you relate with Moses in any way? Share how.

∽ How did God deal with Moses' hesitancy in serving Him? What do you learn from this about God and His ways? How could you apply this knowledge to your own life?

∽ What did you learn about God and your relationship to Him after you read and meditated on the verses in John and Matthew?

THOUGHT FOR THE WEEK

When God calls us for a task, whatever it might be, He is responsible to supply us with whatever we need in order to accomplish His work. The Christian life is one of total dependence and unwavering obedience. While Moses' life clearly demonstrates the importance of living this way, Jesus is our ultimate example. Jesus lived in total dependence upon the Father. The words that He spoke were the Father's words; the works He did were the Father's works.

If you will abide in Jesus, Beloved, and let Jesus and His words abide in you, then you will be prepared for every good work of life. If you are God's child, He tells you that you are "His workmanship, created in Christ Jesus for good works, which God prepared beforehand so that we would walk in them" (Ephesians 2:10).

WEEK THREE

As you read this week, look for and mark the following references in addition to those on your bookmark:

> any reference to the fact that Pharaoh did not listen
>
> any reference to Pharaoh's heart being hardened
>
> the phrase *Let My people go, that they may serve Me*

Then think about what you learn from marking these key repeated phrases.

In the margin of your Bible, for easy reference, make a note of each judgment or plague that God brings upon Pharaoh and/or the people of Egypt.

DAY ONE

Read Exodus 7:1-13.

DAY TWO

Read Exodus 7:14-25.

DAY THREE

Read Exodus 8.

DAY FOUR

Read Exodus 9:1-12.

DAY FIVE

Read Exodus 9:13-35.

DAY SIX

Read Exodus 10.

DAY SEVEN

Store in your heart: Exodus 9:1.

Read and discuss: Exodus 9:13–10:2 and Romans 9:17. Discuss the various purposes of the plagues and their effects.

QUESTIONS FOR DISCUSSION OR INDIVIDUAL STUDY

∾ What were the various plagues that God brought on the land of Egypt? (If you are leading a class discussion, list these on a board if possible.)

∾ Which of these plagues were Pharaoh's men able to duplicate?

∾ As you consider these plagues, what do you learn about God?

∾ List on the board the various gods of Egypt and how they were symbolized. (See the chart on page 60 for this information.) Then examine the plagues God brought with the Egyptian gods and their domain of power and authority.

∽ How did God harden Pharaoh's heart? Did Pharaoh have any part in this at all? What do you learn from comparing what you learn from Exodus with Romans 9:17?

Some of the Gods of Egypt		
The god:	Ruled over:	How symbolized:
Aker	Earth-god • Helper of the dead	Two lion heads
Aton	Sun-god	
Bes	Protection at birth • Dispenser of virility	Group of demons
Heket	Primordial goddess	Frog
Isis	Goddess of life and healing	Human
Khepri	Primordial god • Rising sun	Scarabaeus (beetle)
Khnum	Giver of the Nile • Creator of mankind	Human with ram's head
Mut	"Eye of the sun"	Vulture or human
Nut	Sky goddess • Mother of heavenly bodies	
Osiris	Dead Pharaohs • Ruler of dead, life, vegetation	
Ra	God of sun, earth, and sky • National god	Human with falcon head
Selket	Guardian of life • Protector of dead	Scorpion
Seth	God of chaos, desert and storm, crops	
Sothis	God of Nile floodwaters	
Thermuthis	Goddess of fertility and harvest; fate	Serpent

THOUGHT FOR THE WEEK

Are our hearts not somewhat hardened every time we know to do the will of God but then willfully refuse to do it? Were we not released from sin's slavery that we might serve our Lord Jesus Christ?

Whom are you serving, Beloved? How willingly? How completely?

WEEK FOUR

DAY ONE

Read Exodus 11. Ask the 5 W's and an H about the last plague. List the facts about this plague.

DAY TWO

Read Exodus 12:1-14. Mark every reference to *lamb* and list all you learn regarding the lamb and what was to be done to it, how it was to be done, and when. Also mark the word *blood* and note what you learn about the blood.

DAY THREE

Read Exodus 12:15-28. Mark every occurrence of the word *Passover*.

DAY FOUR

Read Exodus 12:29-39. Compare 12:35,36 with 3:21,22; 11:2,3; Psalm 105:37,38.

DAY FIVE

Read Psalm 105 and note the segment of the psalm that covers the events in the first 12 chapters of Exodus.

DAY SIX

Read Exodus 12:40-51. Compare 12:40,41 with Genesis 15:12-16. Note how long the Israelites lived in Egypt, and how many years of that period were spent in slavery to Pharaoh. List all you learn about the Passover from observing Exodus 12.

DAY SEVEN

Store in your heart: Exodus 12:13.
Read and discuss: Exodus 12:1-20; John 1:29; 1 Corinthians 5:6-8; 1 Peter 1:18,19.

QUESTIONS FOR DISCUSSION OR INDIVIDUAL STUDY

ॐ What were the Israelites to do in order to prepare for the Passover? When were they to do it? Examine the Passover in the light of the 5 W's and an H.

ॐ What feast immediately followed Passover? How important were these feasts to the children of Israel? Why?

ॐ What did these feasts symbolize and/or point to? What, if anything, do they have to do with you? Is there anything here applicable to your life?

∾ What did you learn about God, His character, and His
ways from your study this week?

THOUGHT FOR THE WEEK

Whoever commits sin becomes the slave of sin. But if
the Son shall set you free, you will be free indeed (John
8:34-36). If you belong to Jesus Christ, then you have been
set free from slavery to sin by the blood of God's Passover
Lamb, the Lord Jesus Christ. Now keep "the feast" and "do
not go on presenting the members of your body to sin as
instruments of unrighteousness; but present yourselves to
God as those alive from the dead, and your members as
instruments of righteousness to God" (Romans 6:13).
Make this your daily habit and watch what the Lord does.

WEEK FIVE

DAY ONE

Read Exodus 13:1-16. Mark the word *firstborn* and/or *first offspring* and list all you learn about the firstborn.

DAY TWO

Read Exodus 13:17-22. Compare this with Genesis 50:24-26. Mark your key words.

DAY THREE

Read Exodus 14:1-14. Note carefully how the people again respond to Moses. What principles of leadership can you learn from this?

DAY FOUR

Read Exodus 14:15-31. Note carefully what Moses is told to do and what God does.

DAY FIVE

Read Exodus 15:1-21. Note what you learn about God from this passage. Compare the attitude of the children of Israel in this passage with their attitude as recorded in 14:10-12.

DAY SIX

Read Exodus 15:22-27. Note what you learn about the children of Israel from this passage. Also note what you learn about the Lord.

DAY SEVEN

Store in your heart: Exodus 14:14.

Read and discuss: Exodus 14:10-31; Psalm 106:1-13. Watch the references in this psalm to the fact that the children of Israel did not understand and quickly forgot the ways of the Lord.

QUESTIONS FOR DISCUSSION OR INDIVIDUAL STUDY

- ∾ How did God bring Israel's ultimate deliverance from Pharaoh and the Egyptians?

- ∾ How did this impact the Israelites? For how long?

- ∾ What do you learn from this deliverance about God and the sphere of His power and influence?

- ∾ What do you learn about God and His ways from Exodus 15? What is the Lord in respect to us?

ᴈ As you did your assignments this week, what did you learn about the Israelites? Do you relate to them in any way? How? Why?

THOUGHT FOR THE WEEK

What is our response to difficult situations? Are we quick to remember God's promises, His power, and His faithfulness? Do we see these situations as a test of our faith and respond accordingly? Do we cling to Him in faith, or do we turn to murmur, grumble, and complain—or blame our earthly leaders? How similar are we to the children of Israel?

WEEK SIX

DAY ONE

Read Exodus 16:1-12. Besides marking any words in the text which you have listed on your Exodus bookmark, mark *test* and *grumblings*. Also note carefully the instructions the Lord gave the Israelites regarding gathering the bread from heaven.

DAY TWO

Read Exodus 16:13-36. Make a list of everything you learn regarding the manna.

DAY THREE

Read Deuteronomy 8. Record any new insights you learn regarding the manna and its purpose. Think about how this would apply to you in your walk with the Lord.

DAY FOUR

Read John 6:1-35. Mark the words *sign* and *bread* (*food, manna*). Note the relationship between manna and the bread of life.

DAY FIVE

Read Exodus 17:1-7; 1 Corinthians 10:1-13; John 7:37-39. Mark the words *test* and *tested.* According to these passages, what/who was the rock a picture of, and what was the significance of smiting the rock?

DAY SIX

Read Exodus 17:8-16. Mark the word *staff* and think about all you have learned about Moses' staff and the way it was used. Then meditate on the source of the Israelites' victory.

DAY SEVEN

Store in your heart: 1 Corinthians 10:4.

Read and discuss: Exodus 17:1-7; 1 Corinthians 10:1-4; John 7:37-39. Or read and discuss Exodus 17:8-16, and memorize Exodus 17:15.

QUESTIONS FOR DISCUSSION OR INDIVIDUAL STUDY

∽ How was the "no water" situation a test for the people? What kind of a test was it?

∽ What was the solution to the "no water" situation?

∽ According to the New Testament references you looked up, what did all this picture for us? What did it foreshadow?

ↀ What lessons can you learn from this incident in the life of the Israelites?

ↀ What happens in Exodus 17:8-16? What principles do you see in this passage that you can apply to your own life?

ↀ What have you learned about God and His ways as you have done your study this week?

THOUGHT FOR THE WEEK

In Genesis 22, when God provided the ram in the thicket in the place of Isaac, God revealed Himself as Jehovah (actually YHWH) Jireh—"the Lord will provide." Beloved ones, Jesus Christ, God's rock, has been smitten for you. Everything you will ever need is found in the wellspring of Jesus Christ and your relationship to Him. Even victory over the enemy does not come through the strength of man's flesh. God is Jehovah (YHWH) Nissi, "the Lord your banner." Every "no water" situation, every battle, is a test from God to see where you will turn in the day of trouble.

WEEK SEVEN

DAY ONE

Read Exodus 18 and 19. As you read these chapters examine them in the light of the 5 W's and an H: who, what, when, where, why, and how. What are the main events covered in these chapters? When and where do they occur? etc.

DAY TWO

Read Exodus 20. Number the commandments given in this chapter, noting the various relationships that are affected by obeying or disobeying them.

DAY THREE

Read Exodus 21. Note how God instructed the Israelites to deal with various incidents of violence. Compare Exodus 21:1-6 with Deuteronomy 15:12-18. Note what you learn about becoming a bondservant—a permanent servant to a master.

DAY FOUR

Read Exodus 22. Mark the word *restitution* in this chapter and then note what you learn from marking it. Also watch for the repeated use of *cry* and note what you learn about crying to the Lord.

DAY FIVE

Read Exodus 23. Record what you learn about sabbaths and feasts. Examine them in the light of the 5 W's and an H.

DAY SIX

Read Exodus 24. Mark the following words: *covenant, blood, cloud.* Also note all references to time.

DAY SEVEN

Store in your heart: Mark 12:30,31.
Read and discuss: Exodus 20:1-21; Galatians 3:23-25; Matthew 5:17-20; Romans 8:1-4.

QUESTIONS FOR DISCUSSION OR INDIVIDUAL STUDY

- ❧ Can you list the Ten Commandments as given in Exodus 20?

- ❧ Which of these commandments would it be hard for you to obey and why?

- ❧ From reading Exodus 24, what do you learn about the people's response to these commandments?

෨ As you looked at the New Testament cross-references, what did you learn about the law (the old covenant as inaugurated in Exodus 24)?

෨ Is the Christian allowed to break the law or to live in disregard to it? Or are we in some way to fulfill the law? What is to be our relationship to the law?

THOUGHT FOR THE WEEK

Although we are under the covenant of grace and not law, true Christianity does not condone an ungodly lifestyle. It does not leave us lawless. God calls us to be holy even as He is holy, and gives us the grace with which we can be holy: He gives us the gift of the indwelling Holy Spirit.

Remember Jude's admonition to contend earnestly for the faith which was once for all delivered to the saints, since certain persons have crept in unnoticed, ungodly persons who have turned the grace of God into licentiousness and have denied our only Master and Lord, Jesus Christ (Jude 3,4).

WEEK EIGHT

の〜の〜の〜の

The chapters you read this week will describe the various articles of furniture in the tabernacle and the various parts of the tabernacle. You will also read about the garments that Aaron was to wear as the high priest.

Make a list of each of these. (If you have the *NISB* you will find drawings of these in the margin of the text.) Note where each of the pieces of the furniture was placed in the tabernacle. There is a diagram of the tabernacle below. If you have an *NISB,* you can find a full-color picture of the tabernacle on pages NISB-34-35.

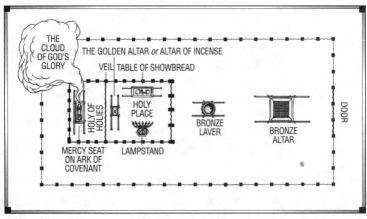

Inside the Tabernacle

DAY ONE

Read Exodus 25.

DAY TWO

Read Exodus 26.

DAY THREE

Read Exodus 27.

DAY FOUR

Read Exodus 28.

DAY FIVE

Read Exodus 29.

DAY SIX

Read Exodus 30 and 31.

DAY SEVEN

Store in your heart: Exodus 25:8.

Read and discuss: Exodus 25:1-9; Hebrews 8:1-6; 9:1-5; 10:19-22. Draw a diagram of the tabernacle and place the furniture in its proper places.

QUESTIONS FOR DISCUSSION OR INDIVIDUAL STUDY

∾ Can you draw a diagram of the tabernacle and its furniture?

∾ How important was the tabernacle? What was its significance to the children of Israel?

∾ From what you studied in the New Testament references, what do you think each piece of furniture in the tabernacle is a picture or foreshadow of?

∾ How does all this apply to us who have put our faith in the Lord Jesus Christ and are now under the new covenant?

∾ What did you learn about God and His ways from this week's study?

THOUGHT FOR THE WEEK

Every piece of the furniture in the tabernacle pointed to the work of our Lord Jesus Christ. Think of how each piece portrayed the life of our Lord. Remember, He is the door, the only way to God (John 10:1,2,7-9). The bronze altar where the animals were sacrificed reminds us of God's Lamb slain for our sins on Calvary's cross. As you move by each piece, pause and worship your Lord and thank Him for who He is and what He has done for you.

WEEK NINE

DAY ONE

Read Exodus 32:1-14. Mark the words listed on your bookmark. List everything you learn from this segment of the chapter about Moses, Aaron, the children of Israel, and God. Leave room to add to each when you finish the chapter.

DAY TWO

Read Exodus 32:15-35. Mark every occurrence of *sin*. Finish the lists you started yesterday and note what you learned about the word *sin*. Read Psalm 106:1-23.

DAY THREE

Read Exodus 33. Mark every reference to the *tent* and *the tent of meeting*. Then list all you learn about this tent and Moses' relationship to it.

DAY FOUR

Read Exodus 33 again. This time ask the 5 W's and an H regarding the content of this chapter.

DAY FIVE

Read Exodus 34. Once again examine the content of this chapter in the light of the 5 W's and an H. Make sure you list all you learn about God from this chapter. Mark the word *covenant*.

DAY SIX

Read 2 Corinthians 3, which contrasts the two covenants: the law or the ministry of condemnation and the new covenant, also referred to as the ministry of righteousness. List what you learn about each. Then note why Moses put a veil over his face.

DAY SEVEN

Store in your heart: Exodus 33:13.

Read and discuss: Exodus 32:1-14 and Exodus 33:7-17. Discuss how Moses responded to the sin of the people and how God offered to destroy them and create a new nation through Moses.

QUESTIONS FOR DISCUSSION OR INDIVIDUAL STUDY

∞ What happened to the children of Israel after Moses was on the mount for 40 days and 40 nights (Exodus 24:18ff.)? Rehearse the course of events.

∞ Discuss Aaron's response to the people and Moses' response to Aaron and the people.

∾ What do you learn about Moses when God offers to make of Moses a great nation? What do you learn about Moses' relationship with God from Exodus 33?

∾ What do you learn about God and His ways as you observe His dealings with the children of Israel and Moses in these chapters?

∾ If God is the same yesterday, today, and forever, what can you apply to your life? What have you learned from Moses' example?

∾ Do you meet with God? How often? Is it adequate? What difference has it made in your life and your relationships?

THOUGHT FOR THE WEEK

Have you ever thought of making the Word of God your "tent of meeting"? As you spend time in God's presence, in His Word, you will learn His ways and come to know Him more intimately and thus find favor in His sight.*

---

* This is why we at Precept Ministries expend ourselves to make *The New Inductive Study Bible* available in every language that God makes possible.

We believe the reason God brought this unique study Bible into existence is so that anyone (who can read) can feed himself from the Word of God for the rest of his or her life.

Through following simple instructions, you can discover for yourself what the Word of God says apart from notes that seek to espouse a particular view of the text.

WEEK TEN

As you read each chapter this week, mark any key words listed on your bookmark as they appear in the text. Also mark the phrase *he made* or *they made*. Note what was made and its purpose.

DAY ONE

Read Exodus 35.

DAY TWO

Read Exodus 36.

DAY THREE

Read Exodus 37.

DAY FOUR

Read Exodus 38.

DAY FIVE

Read Exodus 39.

DAY SIX

Read Exodus 40.

DAY SEVEN

Store in your heart: Exodus 40:36,38.

Read and discuss: Exodus 40:34-38; 2 Chronicles 5:1,2, 7,13–6:1; John 7:37-39; 14:16-18; 16:7-13; 1 Corinthians 3:16; 6:19,20; Romans 8:9.

QUESTIONS FOR DISCUSSION OR INDIVIDUAL STUDY

- From all the references that you have looked up today, where has God dwelt in the glory of His presence? Does He have a temple now to dwell in? Explain your answer from the Word.

- God once led the children of Israel by a cloud. How does He lead His people now?

- Where is the Spirit of God in relationship to every child of God?

- How are we to live in the light of these truths? Are we doing so?

- What are the most significant things you have learned from your study of Exodus about God and His ways? Has it had any effect on your relationship with God? What effect?

THOUGHT FOR THE WEEK

God desires an intimate relationship with His people, for He is not a God who is far off. Thus Moses built a tabernacle after the pattern of God's throne in heaven, and God filled that tabernacle with the glory of His presence.

Then Solomon built a temple, and once again the glory of the Lord abode there until the days of Ezekiel and the Babylonian captivity.

After the 70 years of captivity the remnant of Israel returned, and in 516 B.C. they completed the second temple. But the glory of the Lord never filled that temple until God tabernacled with men in the presence of His beloved Son, our Lord Jesus Christ.

Then just before His crucifixion, Jesus walked out of the temple. Once again the glory of the Lord had departed.

But God still desired an intimate relationship with His people. Thus after Jesus ascended to the Father, at the feast of Pentecost, God sent His Holy Spirit to indwell those who received the Lord Jesus Christ as their Lord and Savior.

If you know Jesus Christ, then you have been delivered from Egypt, from the world, and are never to return. As the children of Israel were delivered from bondage as slaves to Pharaoh, so you have been delivered from Satan's kingdom of darkness, from the prince of this world. You are no longer slaves of sin, for the Son has set you free. You have become a temple of the living God. Beloved, may everything in His temple say "Glory to the Lord." Keep on being filled with His blessed Holy Spirit!

EXODUS AT A GLANCE

Theme of Exodus:

SEGMENT DIVISIONS

Author:				CHAPTER THEMES
Historical Setting:				1
				2
Purpose:				3
				4
Key Words: *(including synonyms)*				5
				6
				7
				8
				9
				10
				11
				12
				13
				14
				15
				16
				17
				18
				19
				20

EXODUS AT A GLANCE

SEGMENT DIVISIONS

			CHAPTER THEMES
			21
			22
			23
			24
			25
			26
			27
			28
			29
			30
			31
			32
			33
			34
			35
			36
			37
			38
			39
			40

LEVITICUS

LEVITICUS
BE HOLY EVEN AS I AM HOLY...

∾∾∾∾

Leviticus! While the thought of studying Leviticus may not seem thrilling to you, once you get into this rich book you will be delightfully surprised. You will learn much about God, and in doing so you will understand why forsaking sin and living a holy life is critical to your well-being and an abiding sense of peace, and thus to true contentment.

This is a book which could be used of God to bring revival in your life and in your church. In Leviticus you will come face-to-face with sin and its awful ramifications, and if you listen you will come away with a holy fear of God—a reverential trust and respect that will bring cleansing and new intimacy to your relationship with your Father God.

GENERAL INSTRUCTIONS

As you study Leviticus there are several key words you will want to mark all the way through the book. Write these on a card that you can use as a bookmark. Then color each word on your bookmark in a distinctive way—the way you want to mark it in your Bible.

> *the Lord spoke to Moses saying*
> *tabernacle (tent of meeting)*
> *law*
> *sacrifice (offering)*
> *sin (iniquity)*
> *blood*
> *holy*
> *covenant*
> *atonement*

Record the main theme of each chapter on the LEVITICUS AT A GLANCE chart (page 114). Then when you finish you will always have a synopsis of Leviticus right at your fingertips. You may also want to record the theme by the chapter number in your Bible.

Record what you learn about each of the offerings by making a chart with these headings: THE OFFERING;

CHAPTER/VERSE; VOLUNTARY/INVOLUNTARY; REA-
SON/PURPOSE. Filling in your chart will give you a permanent synopsis of each of the offerings, all on one page.

WEEK ONE

This week you are going to read about the various offerings. As you do so, examine each offering in the light of the 5 W's and an H. For example, ask such questions as: "What is the offering? What is to be offered? What is done to it? Who is to offer it? Why is it to be offered? When? How?" While you may not find all the answers to your questions, you will see all that God deems important.

DAY ONE

Read Exodus 40:17,32-38 and Leviticus 1:1,2 to see the uninterrupted flow from Exodus to Leviticus. Then read Leviticus 1. Mark the phrase *burnt offering*.

DAY TWO

Read Leviticus 2. Mark every occurrence of *grain offering*.

DAY THREE

Read Leviticus 3. Mark every occurrence of *peace offerings*.

DAY FOUR

Read Leviticus 4. Mark every occurrence of *sin offering.* Also mark *sin* and *unintentionally.* As you read, note the "whos"—i.e., priests, leaders, congregation, etc.

DAY FIVE

Read Leviticus 5. Mark the word *guilt.* Also watch for the word *restitution* and note what restitution is to be made and when.

DAY SIX

Read Leviticus 6. Mark the word *restitution.* Also note the laws of the various offerings.

DAY SEVEN

Store in your heart: Leviticus 5:17.
Read and discuss: Leviticus 5:14–6:7; Ezekiel 33:10-16.

QUESTIONS FOR DISCUSSION OR INDIVIDUAL STUDY

∾ What have you learned about sin this week? If our sin is unintentional, are we still responsible for it?

∾ What was God's provision for dealing with the people's sins?

∾ How important was restitution? To whom was restitution to be made? How was it to be made?

∾ Why would restitution be important?

∾ Do you think a Christian should make restitution? Why? Is there any Scripture that you know that would support or contradict your position on restitution?

THOUGHT FOR THE WEEK

Whether committed willfully or unintentionally, sin has consequences. To ask God and the one whom you have sinned against for forgiveness is only right. However, our genuine sorrow for that sin is shown to man not merely by confession and asking forgiveness but by *restitution* if it affected that person in some sort of a material or tangible way.

Is there anyone to whom you should make restitution? To do so may be costly to you, but remember how costly it was first to Jesus Christ, and then to the one you transgressed against. What else can you do?

Week Two

DAY ONE

Read Leviticus 7. Mark the reference to the laws of the various offerings.

DAY TWO

Read Leviticus 8. Note carefully all that is done to Aaron and his sons.

DAY THREE

Read 1 Peter 1:13–2:10. Mark these words: *holy, obedient (obedience), priesthood, spiritual sacrifices.*

DAY FOUR

Read Leviticus 9. Watch carefully how Aaron and his sons were to offer the sacrifices. Also mark *the glory of the Lord.*

DAY FIVE

Read Leviticus 10:1-7. Note what you learn about God. You might want to record it in the margin of your Bible.

DAY SIX

Read Leviticus 10:8-20. Once again note what you learn about God. However, also watch how Aaron and Moses deal with one another. Note what you learn about leadership.

DAY SEVEN

Store in your heart: Leviticus 10:3.

Read and discuss: Leviticus 10; 1 Peter 2:4-10; Revelation 1:5,6.

QUESTIONS FOR DISCUSSION OR INDIVIDUAL STUDY

∽ Why did God say that Nadab and Abihu, the sons of Aaron, did not treat Him as holy? What did they do and what were the consequences?

∽ What did you learn from the chapters you studied this week about the priesthood?

∽ According to the New Testament passages you studied, who are priests today and what does God expect from them?

∽ What did you learn this week about God and His ways?

∾ Does the way you live show God's calling on your life to be a priest unto God? What do you need to do?

Thought for the Week

God puts His children into the priesthood. Priests offer sacrifices. In the light of all that the Father, Son, and Holy Spirit did for us in bringing us the glorious gospel, should our first sacrifice not be the one called for in Romans 12:1,2? It is truly a reasonable sacrifice.

As priests unto our God, can we live ordinary lives like others? Isn't there a very high and rightful calling upon your life? Remember, "You are a chosen race, a royal priesthood, a holy nation, a people for God's own possession, so that you may proclaim the excellencies of Him who has called you out of darkness into His marvelous light" (1 Peter 2:9). Live accordingly, Beloved.

WEEK THREE

DAY ONE

Read Leviticus 11 and 12. Mark the word *unclean*.

DAY TWO

Read Leviticus 13 and 14. Mark the words *leprosy* and *leper* and note what you learn about leprosy.

DAY THREE

Read Leviticus 15. Mark the words *unclean* and *uncleanness*.

DAY FOUR

Read Leviticus 16. You will study this chapter for the next three days. Therefore on this first reading simply mark the word *atonement*. Also note the major divisions of this chapter.

DAY FIVE

Read Leviticus 16:1-19. Mark the key words on your bookmark. Note what is done with the two goats and how one is selected to be the scapegoat. List what Aaron is to do with the bull and the goat for the sin offering. Consult the diagram of the tabernacle (the tent of meeting) in the section of this book that covers Exodus (page 73).

DAY SIX

Read Leviticus 16:20-34. Mark key words. List what is done to the scapegoat. Also make a list of the basic facts you learn from this chapter about the day of atonement.

DAY SEVEN

 Store in your heart: Leviticus 16:30.
Read and discuss: Leviticus 16:29-34; Hebrews 9:6-15.

QUESTIONS FOR DISCUSSION OR INDIVIDUAL STUDY

ை What was the procedure the high priest was to go through on the day of atonement? If you have a whiteboard, draw a diagram of the tabernacle (see page 73) and visually walk the class through the procedure as they tell it to you.

ை What do you think the procedure with the two goats pictures in respect to the atonement of sin?

ை How does all of this compare with Jesus' sacrifice for our sins? What did you learn from Hebrews 9?

∾ What assurance does this give you in respect to your own sin?

∾ What does all this tell you about God?

THOUGHT FOR THE WEEK

To those who walk in faith, who take God at His Word, the burden of our sins is gone. We are living on this side of the cross. We are partakers of the new covenant. Jesus Christ entered the holy place in heaven to appear in the presence of God for us. He is our sin offering, our "scapegoat." And His blood cleanses us from all sin. If we have been born again of the Spirit, we have been "sanctified through the offering of the body of Jesus Christ once for all" (Hebrews 10:10). This is why there is no condemnation to those who are in Christ Jesus.

If, because of your sins, you feel like a second-class citizen in the kingdom of heaven, then put away those feelings and walk in faith. Without faith it is impossible to please God. Those who come to Him must believe that He is, and that He is a rewarder of those who diligently seek Him.

Don't live as if the new covenant never happened; don't remember your sins year after year.

WEEK FOUR

DAY ONE

Read Leviticus 17 and Hebrews 9:22. Mark the word *blood* and note what you learn.

DAY TWO

Read Leviticus 18. Mark the word *nakedness*. List what you learn about sexual sins, including what happens to those who defile themselves in this way.

DAY THREE

Read Leviticus 19. Mark the words *neighbor* and *love*. Note what you learn. Also mark in a distinctive way every reference to anything that has to do with the occult.

DAY FOUR

Read Leviticus 20. Once again mark every reference to anything referring to the occult. Then list all you learn from Leviticus 19 and 20 regarding this subject. As you read, also define the various types of sexual sin described in this chapter. Note how God told the Israelites to deal with the people who sin in this way.

DAY FIVE

Read Leviticus 21. List the various regulations for priests.

DAY SIX

Read Leviticus 22. Note what God says regarding the giving of holy gifts or offerings to the Lord. Then read Malachi 1:6-14.

DAY SEVEN

Store in your heart: Leviticus 20:10 or 20:13.

Read and discuss: Leviticus 20:10-22; Proverbs 5:15-23; Romans 1:25-27; 1 Corinthians 6:18-20.

QUESTIONS FOR DISCUSSION OR INDIVIDUAL STUDY

∞ What are the various types of sexual sin which are mentioned in Leviticus? List them and then note and discuss how each sin is to be handled according to the Word of God.

∞ What are the consequences of sexual sin on a nation and an individual?

∽ What did you learn from Proverbs 5 regarding the relationship of a man and wife, and the violation of this relationship?

∽ What is sexual sin a manifestation of according to Romans 1:25-27, and what are the consequences of such sin?

∽ According to the passages you have studied, is homosexuality a hereditary condition or a willful transgression of God's ways and God's laws? Explain the reason you answer the way you do.

∽ In the light of what you have seen this week, what do you think about teaching "safe sex"? Why?

THOUGHT FOR THE WEEK

God's commandments and instructions regarding sexual sin are very clear. His warnings regarding the consequences of our disobedience to His known will are there for all to read. When people or a nation disobey and reap the consequences, they are without excuse.

God has recorded this in His Word:

> Marriage is to be held in honor among all, and the marriage bed is to be undefiled; for fornicators and adulterers God will judge....God has not called us for the purpose of impurity, but in sanctification. So he who rejects this is not rejecting man but the God who gives His Holy Spirit to you (Hebrews 13:4; 1 Thessalonians 4:7,8).

Beloved, if you are His child, you have the power, the ability, and the motive to say no to every form of sexual sin. Don't reap the consequences of disobedience, for you can be sure "your sin will find you out."

WEEK FIVE

DAY ONE

Read Leviticus 23. This chapter sets forth the holy convocations or appointed times (feasts) that were to be kept by the sons of Israel. As you read the chapter see if you can distinguish what these holy convocations were.

DAY TWO

At the end of this segment on Leviticus you will find a chart, THE FEASTS OF ISRAEL (pages 112–113). As you do your assignments this week and next, you will want to consult this chart.

Understanding the feasts will also make you appreciate the Gospels, since they make repeated references to the feasts.

Read Leviticus 23:1-3; Genesis 2:1-3; Exodus 20:8-11; Exodus 31:12-17. List all you learn about the Sabbath from these passages. You may want to write these cross-references in your Bible next to Leviticus 23:1-3.

DAY THREE

Read Leviticus 23:4,5 and Exodus 12:1-14. Tomorrow you will also look at some other passages that refer to the

Passover. However, at this point list what you learn about this feast from these passages.

DAY FOUR

Read Exodus 12:21-27; John 2:13-22; 13:1-7; 1 Corinthians 5:7. Add to your list what you learn regarding the Passover and its prophetic significance. In other words, what did the Passover point to?

DAY FIVE

Read Leviticus 23:6-8 and 1 Corinthians 5:7,8. List what you learn regarding the feast of unleavened bread and what this feast pointed to.

DAY SIX

Read Leviticus 23:9-14; 1 Corinthians 15:20-23; Matthew 27:50-53. Record what you learn about first fruits and the feast of First Fruits. Think about how these cross-references explain the prophetic significance of the feast of first fruits.

DAY SEVEN

Store in your heart: 1 Corinthians 5:7,8.

Read and discuss: If you studied Exodus, review Exodus 12:1-20. Then read and discuss 1 Corinthians 15:1-3,12-26.

QUESTIONS FOR DISCUSSION OR INDIVIDUAL STUDY

∽ What were the first three feasts called that comprised the feast of Passover?

∽ What did each of the feasts symbolize at the time? What do you think leaven symbolized?

∽ If Jesus died and was raised "according to the Scriptures," how would the three feasts of Passover show the death and resurrection of Jesus Christ?

∽ What was Paul appealing to in 1 Corinthians 5, when he mentioned the feasts? What was he calling the church at Corinth to? Why?

∽ How do you live in respect to Christ's sin offering for you? Are you "keeping the feast"?

THOUGHT FOR THE WEEK

The feasts were given to the sons of Israel, foreshadowing what and who was to come. They were to keep these feasts faithfully, celebrating them year after year. But now, at the end of the ages, the shadow has been replaced by the substance.

And what are we to do? We are to live in the light of the reality of their fulfillment. We have been set free from sin's slavery by the blood of our Passover Lamb, the Lord Jesus Christ. Now we are to continually keep the feast by putting away sin, keeping the feast with the unleavened bread of sincerity and truth. How close is your life to truth? How sincere is your Christianity? Are you walking in the newness of your resurrected life? As we "have borne the image of the earthy [Adam], we will also bear the image of the heavenly [Jesus Christ]" (1 Corinthians 15:49). Whose image do you portray to the world around you? Keep the feast, Beloved! Lost people must see and sense the difference so they will want the One we have!

WEEK SIX

DAY ONE

Read Leviticus 23:15-21 and Acts 2. Record all you learn about the feast of Pentecost and its prophetic significance.

DAY TWO

Read John 7:37-39; Galatians 3:13-15; Ephesians 1:13,14; 1 Corinthians 12:13. Note how these show the fulfillment of Pentecost. For the symbolism of the two loaves of bread (Leviticus 23:17) look at Ephesians 2:11-22; 3:6.

DAY THREE

Read Leviticus 23:23-25; Isaiah 11:12; Matthew 24:31; Ezekiel 36:24. Record what you learn regarding the feast of trumpets and its yet-to-be-fulfilled prophetic significance.

DAY FOUR

Read Leviticus 23:26-32 and Ezekiel 36:25-27. List what you learn regarding the day of atonement. Remember all you learned from Leviticus 16. Since the nation of Israel did not recognize Jesus as the Passover Lamb who took away the sins of the world in His first coming, does the day of atonement point prophetically to the day when all Israel will be saved (Romans 11:26,27)?

DAY FIVE

Read Leviticus 23:33-44 and John 7:2,37-39. Note what you learn regarding the feast of tabernacles (or booths), and then note what Jesus did at the celebration of this feast.

DAY SIX

Read Zechariah 14. Note the events that will lead up to the yet-future celebration of the feast of booths as mentioned in Zechariah 14:16-21. Also read Ezekiel 36:28,38; 37:26-28.

DAY SEVEN

Store in your heart: John 7:37-39.
Read and discuss: Leviticus 23:15-34; John 7:37-39; Acts 2:1-4,16-18,38,39; Ephesians 2:11-22; 3:4-6. If there is time, discuss the significance of all the feasts you studied this week.

QUESTIONS FOR DISCUSSION OR INDIVIDUAL STUDY

∽ What was the procedure the Israelites were to follow at the feast of Pentecost? List everything they were to do, then note the number of loaves of bread and what the bread was made of. How does this compare with the feast of Passover?

∾ What happened at the feast of Pentecost in Acts 2?

∾ How does this relate with Jesus' promise in John 7:37-39?

∾ How does it relate to the verses you studied in chapters 2 and 3 of Ephesians?

∾ What was the feast of Pentecost a picture or foreshadower of?

∾ When you study the feasts, what do you learn about God, His Word, and His ways?

THOUGHT FOR THE WEEK

In Romans 11:25-29 Paul writes,

> For I do not want you, brethren, to be uninformed of this mystery—so that you will not be wise in your own estimation—that a partial hardening has happened to Israel until the fulness of the Gentiles has come in; and so all Israel will be saved; just as it is written, "The Deliverer will come from Zion, He will remove ungodliness from Jacob. This is My covenant with them, when I take away their sins." From the standpoint of the gospel they are enemies for your sake, but from the standpoint of God's choice they are beloved for the sake of the fathers; for the gifts and the calling of God are irrevocable.

According to these verses God is not finished with the nation of Israel. Could it be that in Christ's first coming we have seen the fulfillment of the first four feasts, through Pentecost? Could it be that those who have believed in Jesus Christ have reaped the prophetic benefits of these feasts, but that there remain three other feasts—Trumpets, Atonement, and Booths—which we will not see fulfilled until the second coming of Christ, when Israel as a nation will recognize Jesus Christ as the Messiah?

Think about it: How far away is this fulfillment? Be on the alert, Beloved, for He will come like a thief in the night. Be ready!

WEEK SEVEN

❧❧❧❧

DAY ONE

Read Leviticus 24:1-16,23 and Exodus 20:7. Note what it means to take the Lord's name in vain.

DAY TWO

Read Leviticus 24:17-23; Exodus 21:22-29; Genesis 9:5,6; Matthew 5:38-42. Note what you learn about the value of a life. Also note how the law restrained the injured party from acting in unrestrained vengeance.

DAY THREE

Read Leviticus 25:1-22. Mark these words: *jubilee, land,* and *sabbath.* List all you learn about the year of jubilee. Then read Leviticus 25:23-38 and list what you learn regarding the redemption of the land, and why it was to be redeemed.

DAY FOUR

Read Leviticus 25:39-55. Mark these words: *jubilee, land, kinsman (relative), redemption (redeem).* List what you learn regarding the redemption of a kinsman.

DAY FIVE

Read Leviticus 26 and 27. Mark *covenant, idol(s), land, sabbaths,* and the phrase *seven times for your sins.* Then list the consequences of obedience and disobedience.

DAY SIX

Read Leviticus 27 and Matthew 5:33-37. Mark *vows, consecrates (sets apart),* and *value it (valuation),* and then note what you learn about the importance of vows.

DAY SEVEN

Store in your heart: Leviticus 26:13,46.
Read and discuss: Leviticus 26:1-17,40-46.

QUESTIONS FOR DISCUSSION OR INDIVIDUAL STUDY

∾ According to Leviticus 26, what would God do if the children of Israel obeyed Him? And what would be the consequences if they did not? List your answers in two columns. As you do so, note the degree of judgment that would come because of their sins.

∾ What did you learn from marking the word *covenant?*

∾ As you have studied this week, what have you learned about God and His ways with the children of Israel?

∾ Do you think God can overlook disobedience in the life of a Christian? What did you learn about God that would be applicable to your life today?

∾ How tolerant are you in regard to sin in your own life? In what specific ways has the Lord spoken to you through His Word? What are you doing about what He has said?

THOUGHT FOR THE WEEK

It seems that our generation hears more about our happiness than it does God's holiness. Are we being deceived and sidetracked by pursuing *our* happiness rather than *His* holiness?

Leviticus reveals to us the mind and heart of God in regard to our relationship to Him, to others, and to sin.

God's character and ways do not alter: "'I am the Alpha and the Omega,' says the Lord God, 'who is and who was and who is to come, the Almighty'" (Revelation 1:8).

This is the One who says, "Like the Holy One who called you, be holy yourselves also in all your behavior; because it is written, 'YOU SHALL BE HOLY, FOR I AM HOLY'" (1 Peter 1:15,16).

This is the One who tells us in the book of Hebrews, "Pursue peace with all men, and the sanctification [holiness] without which no one will see the Lord" (12:14).

Now that you have studied Leviticus and seen what the Word of God says, will you pursue your happiness or His holiness? The choice is yours, but you do not choose the consequences. Remember that.

If you genuinely want to see revival come to your life, your church, and your nation, remember that it has always come when the children of God decided to deal thoroughly with their sin—not to cover it, but to confess and forsake it. Then the Spirit of God broke through and reached those who did not know Him.

Revival begins with the pursuit of God, and the pursuit of God leads to true holiness.

THE FEASTS OF ISRAEL

	1st Month (Nisan) Festival of Passover (Pesach)				3rd Month (Sivan) Festival of Pentecost (Shavuot)
Slaves in Egypt	**Passover**	**Unleavened Bread**	**First Fruits**		**Pentecost or Feast of Weeks**
	Kill lamb & put blood on doorpost Exodus 12:6, 7	*Purging of all leaven* (symbol of sin)	*Wave offering of sheaf* (promise of harvest to come)		*Wave offering of two loaves of leavened bread*
Whosoever commits sin is the slave to sin	1st month, 14th day Leviticus 23:5	1st month, 15th day for 7 days Leviticus 23:6-8 *(1st and 7th days are Sabbath)*	Day after Sabbath Leviticus 23:9-14 *(It is a Sabbath)*		50 days after first fruits Leviticus 23:15-21 *(It is a Sabbath)*
	Christ our Passover has been sacrificed	**Clean out old leaven... just as you are in fact unleavened**	**Christ has been raised...the first fruits**	**Going away so Comforter can come**	**Promise of the Spirit, mystery of church: Jews-Gentiles in one body**
				 Mount of Olives	
John 8:34	1 Corinthians 5:7	1 Corinthians 5:7, 8	1 Corinthians 15:20-23	John 16:7 Acts 1:9-12	Acts 2:1-47 1 Corinthians 12:13 Ephesians 2:11-22

Months: Nisan—*March, April* • **Sivan**—*May, June* • **Tishri**—*September, October*

7th Month (Tishri)

Festival of Tabernacles *(Succoth)*

	Feast of Trumpets	Day of Atonement	Feast of Booths or Tabernacles	
Interlude Between Festivals	*Trumpet blown — a holy convocation*	*Atonement shall be made to cleanse you* Leviticus 16:30	*Harvest celebration memorial of tabernacles in wilderness*	**New heaven and new earth**
	7th month, 1st day Leviticus 23:23-25 *(It is a Sabbath)*	7th month, 10th day Leviticus 23:26-32 *(It is a Sabbath)*	7th month, 15th day, for 7 days; 8th day, Holy Convocation Leviticus 23:33-44 *(The 1st and 8th days are Sabbaths)*	**God tabernacles with men**
	Regathering of Israel in preparation for final day of atonement Jeremiah 32:37-41	**Israel will repent and look to Messiah in one day** Zechariah 3:9,10; 12:10; 13:1; 14:9	**Families of the earth will come to Jerusalem to celebrate the Feast of Booths** Zechariah 14:16-19	Revelation 21:1-3
		Coming of Christ		
	Ezekiel 36:24	Ezekiel 36:25-27 Hebrews 9, 10 Romans 11:25-29	Ezekiel 36:28	

Israel had two harvests each year—spring and autumn

LEVITICUS AT A GLANCE

Theme of Leviticus:

Author:

Historical Setting:

Purpose:

Key Words:
(including synonyms)

LAWS REGARDING	MAIN DIVISION		CHAPTER THEMES
	WORSHIPING A HOLY GOD	1	
		2	
		3	
		4	
		5	
		6	
		7	
		8	
		9	
		10	
		11	
		12	
		13	
		14	
		15	
		16	
		17	
	LIVING A HOLY LIFE	18	
		19	
		20	
		21	
		22	
		23	
		24	
		25	
		26	
		27	

NUMBERS

NUMBERS
THESE THINGS HAPPENED AS AN EXAMPLE TO US...

ᏧᏧᏧᏧ

Numbers begins just like its name—with numbers. However, it soon turns to the historical account of the people whom God numbered. And when it does so, there are some very valuable lessons to be learned by the child of God: "For whatever was written in earlier times was written for our instruction, that through perseverance and the encouragement of the Scriptures we might have hope" (Romans 15:4).

If you will persevere through the first chapters of Numbers, you will find the Word doing its work—discerning the thoughts and intents of your heart, cleansing you, and bringing you into a greater understanding of the One you call Father.

General Instructions

As you read through Numbers there are certain key repeated words you will want to mark in a distinctive way so you can easily see them as they appear in the text. Write these on an index card that you can cut and use as a bookmark. Color and/or mark the words on the bookmark in the same way you plan to mark them in your Bible.

The words and phrases are:

> *number (census)*
> *the Lord spoke to*
> *service*
> *cloud*
> *wilderness*
> *tent (tabernacle)*
> *war*

Also mark the phrase *of the sons of*_____. Then underline whose sons they were.

WEEK ONE

~~~~~

DAY ONE

Read Numbers 1 and 2. Note the setting of Numbers 1:1. Look at Exodus 40:17 and Numbers 1:1 and you will see one month elapsed between the close of Exodus and the beginning of Numbers. Leviticus covers a period of only one month.

When you read Numbers 2, turn to page 119 to see the camp arrangement.

As you read the first two chapters of Numbers, every time you come to *the sons of* _____ and one of the tribes of Israel is mentioned, highlight or mark that phrase so you can quickly distinguish what is said regarding each tribe.

Mark every reference to the Levites and list what you learn about them from the text. Also look for any other key repeated phrases you might want to mark.

Record the main theme of each chapter on the NUMBERS AT A GLANCE chart (page 139). When you finish, you will have a synopsis of Numbers which you can consult at any time. You may also want to record the theme by the chapter number in your Bible.

DAY TWO

Read Numbers 3 and 4. Mark every reference to the Levites, and in another distinctive way mark the word *first-born*.

Note the names of the three sons of Levi. Then as you read about each of the sons note what their specific duties were. This information will help you understand why God moves in judgment at specific times.

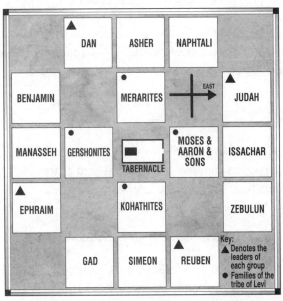

Camp Arrangement of Israel's Tribes

DAY THREE

Read Numbers 5. Mark these words: *unfaithful, jealous (jealousy)*. Note the various laws in this chapter and what they concern.

DAY FOUR

Read Numbers 6. Mark every occurrence of *Nazirite,* then list what you learn regarding the vow of a Nazirite. Remember that Jesus was a Nazarene, someone from the town of Nazareth, so don't get *Nazirite* mixed up with *Nazarene.*

DAY FIVE

Read Numbers 7. Answer as many of the 5 W's and an H as you can about the offerings to be made by the leaders of Israel.

DAY SIX

Read Numbers 8. Mark every reference to the Levites and once again make a list of what you learn. As you do, remember that they were the priests of Israel.

DAY SEVEN

Store in your heart: Numbers 3:10.
Read and discuss: Numbers 3:1-13; Revelation 1:4-6; 1 Peter 2:9-17.

QUESTIONS FOR DISCUSSION OR INDIVIDUAL STUDY

∽ What did you learn about the firstborn? (List the insights on the board.)

∽ What group of people were to be a replacement for the firstborn? What were they called to do? Could anyone else do what they were called to do? (You will see how helpful all of this is when you study other portions of the Scriptures.)

∽ What were the names of the three sons of Levi? What were the particular duties of these three sons?

∽ What parallels do you see between the Old Testament priest and how God refers to those who have believed in the Lord Jesus Christ?

∽ What did you learn about believers when you studied 1 Peter 2:9-17? If you applied these truths to your life how would it affect the way you live?

THOUGHT FOR THE WEEK

Like the Levites, we are the Lord's, a kingdom of priests unto our God. Our main occupation and concern should be to properly worship our God in every aspect of our lives. Whether we eat or drink, or whatever we do, we should do all to the honor and glory of our God.

WEEK TWO

ᕗᕗᕗᕗ

DAY ONE

Read Numbers 9. Note when the Lord is speaking, to whom, and where. Put a time symbol, perhaps a clock, in the margin of your Bible next to 9:1. Mark the words *Passover* and *cloud*. List the instructions regarding the cloud.

DAY TWO

Read Numbers 10. Mark the key words on your bookmark. Give special attention to the cloud, for something significant happens in this chapter. As you read, examine this chapter in the light of the 5 W's and an H.

DAY THREE

Numbers 10:11 began the journeyings of Israel, which were to last for 39 years. This period of time is covered through Numbers 21:35.

Read Numbers 11. There is much to see in this chapter. List the main characters and note what you learn regarding them. Also watch what you learn about God and how He deals with the Israelites.

Record your insights about Moses in your notebook. You began this list if you studied Exodus first. Remember to record lessons for your life that you learn from the life of Moses. If you do this you will always have valuable information you can share with others as the Lord gives you opportunity.

DAY FOUR

Read Numbers 12. List what you learn from this chapter about Moses, Aaron, Miriam, and God.

DAY FIVE

Read Numbers 13. As you read this chapter consult the map on page 124. Mark the word *land* and record all you learn about the land. Ask the 5 W's and an H regarding the land. Note what the spies say and how the people respond.

DAY SIX

Read Numbers 14. Mark every reference to Moses, Joshua, and Caleb, and then see what you learn about these men. Also note what you learn about God and about the people. Don't forget to record your insights on Moses.

DAY SEVEN

Store in your heart: Numbers 14:11 or 14:18.
Read and discuss: Numbers 13:30–14:9; 14:28-38.

QUESTIONS FOR DISCUSSION OR INDIVIDUAL STUDY

∾ Why did the children of Israel go in to spy out the land that God had promised them? Who went? What was the land like? What happened as a result of this journey? Discuss the whole event in the light of the 5 W's and an H.

∾ How did the children of Israel respond to the report of the spies? How did Moses and Aaron respond to the children of Israel? What does this tell you about Moses and Aaron?

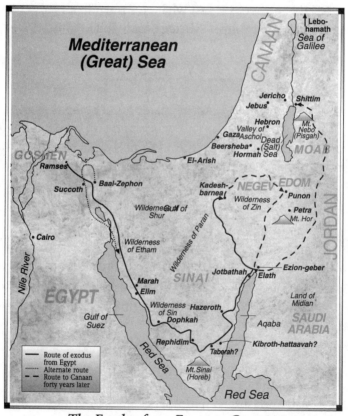

The Exodus from Egypt to Canaan

∾ How did God respond to all this? What do you learn from this incident about God and His ways with His people? Does He ever make distinctions in the ways He deals with people? Why?

∾ What happened to the Israelites? How does this compare with their fears and complaints regarding going into the promised land?

∾ What did you learn that you can apply to your own life? Do you ever respond like the children of Israel, or do you relate more to Joshua, Caleb, and Moses? If it is the latter, what can you expect from the people of God who are moving in the same direction that you are moving?

THOUGHT FOR THE WEEK

Without faith it is impossible to please God; those who come to Him must believe that He is, and that He is God! He is the God of all flesh, the God of the impossible, the God who asks, "Is anything too hard for Me?" He is the God who does according to His will in the army of heaven and among the inhabitants of the earth. He is the God who said, "Call unto me and I will do great and mighty things that you know not."

Wasn't it absolutely insane for the Israelites not to believe Him? How could the Israelites be so foolish as to listen to their fellowman instead of the word of God Almighty?

And to whom do we listen?

WEEK THREE

DAY ONE

Read Numbers 15. Mark the words *unintentionally* and *defiantly*. Then note what you learn from marking each word. Also note the purpose of the tassels. When you go to Israel today you will see many Orthodox Jews wearing prayer shawls under their garments. Sometimes the tassels can be seen hanging out of their waistline or below the bottom of their jackets. Now you know where this practice came from.

DAY TWO

Read Numbers 16. Mark every reference to Korah, Dathan, and Abiram. Record what you learn about each of these men.

DAY THREE

Read Numbers 16 again. Mark the words *grumbled* and *congregation*. Then list all you learn about Moses, God, and the people.

DAY FOUR

Read Numbers 17. Mark the words *rod(s)* (along with any pronouns), *grumbling,* and *sons of Israel.* Note what you learn about Aaron's rod and what was to be done with it.

DAY FIVE

Read Numbers 18. Mark every reference to Levi or the Levites and every reference to the tithe. List what you learn from marking these.

DAY SIX

Read Numbers 19 and Hebrews 9:13-15. Mark the words *ashes* and *heifer.* Then list everything you learn about the ashes of the red heifer.

DAY SEVEN

Store in your heart: 1 Corinthians 10:11,12.
Read and discuss: Numbers 16:1-15,41-50; 1 Corinthians 10:1-6,10; Jude 4,10,11.

QUESTIONS FOR DISCUSSION OR INDIVIDUAL STUDY

∾ What son of Levi did the sons of Korah belong to? What were the duties of this family? Go back to your notes on Numbers 3 and 4 for your answer to this question if you don't remember it.

∾ What was the complaint of the sons of Korah and how did Moses handle it? How did the congregation of the Israelites respond to Moses?

∾ How did God move in this situation? Why? What do you learn about God and His ways from this incident?

∾ How does God use this incident when writing to the church at Corinth? What are the lessons He has for us? How can you apply all this to your own life?

∾ How do the sons of Korah compare with the men described in Jude 4-11,16? What do you learn about rebellion, and how would this apply today?

THOUGHT FOR THE WEEK

God is to be worshiped in His way, not ours. "True worshipers will worship the Father in spirit and truth; for such people the Father seeks to be His worshipers. God is spirit, and those who worship Him must worship in spirit and truth" (John 4:23,24).

Beloved, do you know the truth well enough so that you know if you are worshiping God in truth? Jesus prayed for you, "Sanctify them in the truth; Your word is truth" (John 17:17).

I think that is what is happening as you do this study. I know that it is a battle; Satan will do all he can to keep you from the Word of God. And it is also a battle with your flesh, which can think up all sorts of excuses and reasons for not diligently disciplining yourself to study God's Word. Don't yield to either one. Resist and walk by the Spirit, and then you will know how to worship Him in spirit and truth.

Persevere, Beloved, persevere.

WEEK FOUR

DAY ONE

Read Numbers 20. In addition to the words on your bookmark, mark *rod, rock,* and *water.* Note what you learn regarding Aaron and Moses. Record your insights on Moses. Also note where the events of this passage occur. Pay attention to what you learn about Edom and where the Edomites live. Remember that these are the descendants of Esau (Genesis 25:30). Consult the map on page 124.

DAY TWO

Read Numbers 21 and John 3:14-21. Mark *serpent(s)* and then list what you learn from marking this word. Also observe the journeys of the children of Israel.

DAY THREE

Read Numbers 22. Mark every reference to Balak and to Balaam, and list what you learn about these two men. Also note carefully what the Lord does.

DAY FOUR

Read Numbers 23. Continue to observe Balak and Balaam. Note carefully what Balaam can and cannot do. Note what you learn from this chapter about God and the people of God.

DAY FIVE

Read Numbers 24. Continue to observe Balak and Balaam. Give careful attention to Balaam's oracles and all you learn about God and the people of God.

DAY SIX

Read Numbers 25. Examine the content of this chapter in the light of the 5 W's and an H: who, what, where, why, when, and how. Then read Psalm 106:1-33.

DAY SEVEN

Store in your heart: Numbers 20:12.

Read and discuss: Exodus 17:1-7; 1 Corinthians 10:4; John 7:37-39 (*come* and *drink* in verse 37 are in the present tense and denote habitual action); Numbers 20:1-3.

QUESTIONS FOR DISCUSSION OR INDIVIDUAL STUDY

∾ As you look at all these verses, comparing Scripture with Scripture:

What did the rock symbolize?

What did striking the rock symbolize?

Why was it not necessary to strike the rock a second time?

∾ What happened to Moses and Aaron in Numbers 20? Why?

∾ What do you learn about God from this incident? How does this compare with the other things you have learned about God and His ways as you have studied Genesis, Exodus, and Leviticus? Do you think God has changed? Have His ways changed?

∾ Is there anything you have missed or are missing in life because you have not treated God as holy?

THOUGHT FOR THE WEEK

When you became a child of God by recognizing your sin and impotence to save yourself or to make yourself acceptable in the eyes of God apart from faith in the Lord Jesus Christ and His work on Calvary's cross, you were made complete in Him (Colossians 2:9,10). In Jesus Christ you have everything which pertains to life and godliness (2 Peter 1:2,3). When you turn to other sources—when you rely on the arm of flesh instead of making God your source and strength—do you think this honors God, that this treats Him as holy in the sight of others? Isn't this like striking the Rock a second time, instead of merely speaking to the Rock in prayer? You have not because you ask not!

What blessings does this cause you to miss, Beloved? Think about it, and determine that you will trust Him though He slay you—even as Job did, and as Moses wished he had.

WEEK FIVE

DAY ONE

Read Numbers 26. Don't forget to mark *census* (*numbered*). Also mark *inheritance*. Note what you learn regarding Caleb and Joshua.

DAY TWO

Read Numbers 27. Note what you learn about Moses and Joshua. Record what you learn in this chapter from the way Moses handles the situations of leadership.

DAY THREE

Read Numbers 28. Mark in a distinctive way the different offerings mentioned in this chapter.

DAY FOUR

Read Numbers 29. Again mark the different offerings. Also mark every reference to time.

DAY FIVE

Read Numbers 30. Mark the word *vow* and note what you learn.

DAY SIX

Read Numbers 31. Mark *Midian* (*Midianites*) and *Balaam*. Then note what you learn from marking each reference to these. Also note what was done with the spoils of war as well as what had to be purified and how.

DAY SEVEN

 Store in your heart: Jude 11.

Read and discuss: Numbers 31:1-20; 25:1-9; Revelation 2:14.

QUESTIONS FOR DISCUSSION OR INDIVIDUAL STUDY

∾ Jude talks about the error of Balaam. How would you describe Balaam, and what was his error? (If you have a whiteboard in your classroom, list all that the class can remember about Balaam.)

∾ How was God's wrath turned away from the children of Israel when they played the harlot with the daughters of Moab? What do you learn from this incident? If you have studied Leviticus, how does what happened in Numbers 25 correlate with Leviticus 20 and what God has to say about sexual sin?

∞ What do you learn from Numbers 31 about the consequences of Israel's sin?

∞ Do you see any possible parallel in these accounts relating to Balaam and the children of Israel to what is happening in the world today because of sexual immorality?

∞ Since the things which were written beforehand were written for our learning, what lessons do you think God has for us in all this?

THOUGHT FOR THE WEEK

No one can effectively curse the children of God, for we are blessed by Him. However, when we allow ourselves to be seduced into sin we must come under the discipline of God.

How crucial it is that we diligently examine those who would teach and influence the children of God (and to carefully watch those who would teach us) so that we don't turn the grace of God into lasciviousness and think we can live any way we want and not reap the consequences!

When we sin as children of God, if we do not judge ourselves, then "we are disciplined by the Lord so that we will not be condemned along with the world" (1 Corinthians 11:32).

Woe to those who rush headlong into the error of Balaam!

WEEK SIX

DAY ONE

Read Numbers 32. Mark Reuben, Gad, Manasseh, Joshua, and Caleb, and then note what you learn about each.

DAY TWO

Read Numbers 33. Mark the word *journeyed*. Also note what you learn from this chapter about Aaron and Moses. List God's specific instructions to the sons of Israel when they enter the promised land of Canaan.

DAY THREE

Read Numbers 34. Mark the word *border*. See the map on page 136.

DAY FOUR

Read Numbers 35:1-15. Mark the phrase *cities of refuge*. Note what you learn about the cities for the Levites and the cities of refuge.

DAY FIVE

Read Numbers 35:16-34. Mark *cities of refuge, blood avenger, he is a murderer,* and *the murderer shall be put to death.* Also mark *land* and then note what blood does to the land.

DAY SIX

Read Numbers 36. Mark the word *inheritance.*

Border of Canaan

DAY SEVEN

Store in your heart: Numbers 32:23 or 35:31 or 35:33.

Read and discuss: Genesis 9:5,6; Numbers 35:16-34; Ezekiel 22:1-16. Notice the repeated mention of blood in each of these passages.

QUESTIONS FOR DISCUSSION OR INDIVIDUAL STUDY

∾ What do you learn from all these verses about the sanctity of life?

∾ According to the Word of God, why is the life of a human being so special? Do you know any other Scriptures that would support this?

∾ What were to be the consequences for taking another person's life? How were these consequences to be executed and by whom?

∾ Were there any safeguards? What were they?

∾ According to what you have studied this week, what effect does the shedding of blood have on the land? What can make expiation for the shedding of blood?

∾ What does this tell you about God and His ways? Do you think God has changed? What about His ways— what do you think is a biblical perspective on the death penalty?

∾ How do you think a nation is to govern itself in the light of these truths, or were they only for the nation of Israel?

∾ What do you think would happen if the Word of God were upheld in this matter? Do you think it would change society? Why?

∾ Have you had to adjust any of your beliefs now that you have studied Numbers? What have you learned for your life? What difference will this study make?

THOUGHT FOR THE WEEK

If blood pollutes the land, then where does your nation stand if it does not execute capital punishment or if it legalizes abortion?

If Israel, God's elect nation, did not escape the judgment of God, will your nation?

What have you learned about the value of believing God, of following Him fully as did Caleb and Joshua, even though you have to stand alone?

When God gets ready to number the faithful, to count those who are His valiant warriors and give them their rewards, will you be among those so numbered?

Theme of Numbers:

SEGMENT DIVISIONS

	JOURNEYS/ ENCAMP- MENTS	CHAPTER THEMES	Author:
		1	
		2	*Historical*
		3	*Setting:*
		4	
		5	
		6	
		7	*Purpose:*
		8	
		9	
		10	
		11	*Key Words:*
		12	*(including synonyms)*
		13	
		14	
		15	
		16	
		17	
		18	
		19	
		20	
		21	
		22	
		23	
		24	
		25	
		26	
		27	
		28	
		29	
		30	
		31	
		32	
		33	
		34	
		35	
		36	

DEUTERONOMY

DEUTERONOMY
THIS IS LIFE: LOVING GOD AND OBEYING HIM...

Deuteronomy is the last of the five books which comprise what is known as the Pentateuch. It is God's final word through His faithful servant Moses to the sons of Israel as they prepare to enter the land promised to Abraham, Isaac, Jacob, and his sons for an everlasting possession.

Because Moses did not treat God as holy and struck the rock a second time instead of merely speaking to it, Moses was not allowed to enter the promised land. When he finished rehearsing God's laws, His statutes which were to govern the lives of His people, Moses went up to Mount Nebo and died. Another leader would take the children of Israel across the Jordan River into the land that flowed with milk and honey. Joshua was that new leader.

Of what value is such a study for those who live under the new covenant of grace rather than the old covenant of the law? Untold! The law is holy; it is an expression of the righteousness of God. When we understand it, we understand what displeases our God, and we understand what sin is and how it manifests itself. And we learn how to approach our holy God to find forgiveness and cleansing. The law is the schoolmaster who brings us to Christ. The law tells us how to live.

Why a new covenant then? Because merely *knowing* the law does not enable us to fulfill it. Thus the necessity for a new covenant—a covenant that would not only grant us forgiveness of all our sins for all time but also provide us with One who would enable us to walk in the righteousness of the law. This One is the indwelling Holy Spirit of God. The Spirit is the One who works out our sanctification as we know God's will and walk in it in the power of the Holy Spirit.

Deuteronomy will teach you much about God—His character, His will, His ways. As you observe His relationship with His elect and chosen people, Israel, you will learn much of how you are to live as members of His elect and chosen bride, whom He calls the church.

Study well, Beloved, for what you learn will teach you how to live as His Son lived: He didn't come to nullify the law but to fulfill it, and He did that by living in the power of the Spirit, always and only doing that which pleased the Father. What Jesus saw the Father do, that He did. What the Father spoke, Jesus spoke. The Lord Jesus Christ didn't live a lawless life; He lived a dependent life. He depended totally on the Father. And several times God just had to say, "This is My beloved Son, with whom I am well-pleased."

When Israel got into trouble, it was because they didn't live in the total dependence of obedience, and God said, "How I have been hurt by their adulterous hearts which turned away from Me, and by their eyes which played the harlot after their idols" (Ezekiel 6:9).

May what you learn from Deuteronomy cause you to walk in the power of the Spirit, "by loving the Lord your God, by obeying His voice, and by holding fast to Him, for this is your life." This is the life to which He called you in Christ Jesus your Lord.

WEEK ONE

DAY ONE

Read Deuteronomy 1:1-5. Then, paying attention to people, places, and any reference to time, read Numbers 21:21–22:1 and 36:13; reread Deuteronomy 1:1-5. This will give you the historical setting of Deuteronomy. Mark in a distinctive way all references to time so you can easily spot them.

Record any insights you may gain from these verses on your DEUTERONOMY AT A GLANCE Chart on page 167. You will also want to record each chapter's main theme on this same chart when you begin to work your way through Deuteronomy a chapter at a time.

If you have studied Exodus before beginning this study, you worked on a list of insights you gained from studying the life of Moses. Add any insights you gain as you go through Deuteronomy to this list. If you haven't begun such a list, do so. Be sure to leave yourself plenty of space to add to the list as you study.

DAY TWO

In the first three chapters of Deuteronomy, Moses looks back to the past.

Read Deuteronomy 1. As you read this chapter and the subsequent chapters of Deuteronomy, constantly interrogate the text of each chapter with the 5 W's and an H: who, what, when, where, why, and how. Ask these questions about the main characters, events, or teachings given in the chapter. You will learn much. Record anything you want to remember in the margin of your Bible.

You will also gain some valuable "Lessons For Life" as you study. If you want to remember them, simply put "LFL" in the margin of your Bible and record what you learned that will help you live a life pleasing to your Father God.

Make a list on a five-by-seven card which you can use as a bookmark of the following key repeated words in Deuteronomy. Then color code each of these in a distinctive way on the card, and then in your Bible as you see the occurrence of the word.

The key words to look for throughout Deuteronomy are:

> *then* (this is a time phrase that will help you see the sequences of events in Deuteronomy)
> *fear*
> *heart*
> *command (commanding, commanded)*
> *commandments (statutes)*
> *listen*
> *observe (keep, do)*
> *love*
> *remember*
> *covenant*

DAY THREE

Read Deuteronomy 2 and do the same things you did with chapter 1.

DAY FOUR

Read Deuteronomy 3 and continue your work.

DAY FIVE

Read Deuteronomy 4. Note the change with the phrase, "Now, O Israel, listen...." This begins a new segment which runs through chapter 11.

Over the next weeks as you read chapter by chapter through the eleventh chapter, keep in mind the 5 W's and an H. You will see words such as *when, then, watch, hear, listen, beware,* and *you shall therefore.* When you work in chapters 6, 7, and 9, and see the word *when,* see if *then* eventually follows it. If so, circle the *when* and *then* and connect them with a line. Watch what the people were to do, and what God did.

Record the main points of each chapter in the margin, or underline and note them in the text and number them 1, 2, 3, etc.

DAY SIX

Read Deuteronomy 5. Follow the instructions given yesterday.

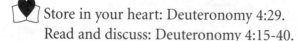
DAY SEVEN

Store in your heart: Deuteronomy 4:29.
Read and discuss: Deuteronomy 4:15-40.

QUESTIONS FOR DISCUSSION OR INDIVIDUAL STUDY

∞ What were the children of Israel to watch carefully? List all the things they were to be careful about and why (if the text tells you).

∞ Next to that list write down the consequences of not "watching carefully." As you think about the history of Israel, did any of these consequences come to pass? How? When? Have they stopped?

∞ What had God done for the children of Israel? Why had He done it?

∞ Why was God angry with Moses?

∞ What do you learn about God from these first five chapters of Deuteronomy?

THOUGHT FOR THE WEEK

Are you in distress, Beloved, because you did not watch yourself so that you lived in total obedience and dependence upon the Lord? Are you doomed to live in your distress and misery for the rest of your life, worth nothing to God and to His kingdom? From wherever you are, seek Him, searching for Him with all your heart and your soul.

> When you are in distress and all these things have come upon you...you will return to the Lord your God and listen to His voice. For the Lord your God is a compassionate God; He will not fail you nor destroy you nor forget the covenant (Deuteronomy 4:30,31).

> He will never leave you nor forsake you, so that you can boldly say, "The Lord is my helper" (from Hebrews 13:5,6).

WEEK TWO

As you read each chapter follow the same instructions you were given last week.

DAY ONE

Read Deuteronomy 6. This chapter contains the famous Jewish "Shema" (pronounced Sh'ma) in verse 4.

DAY TWO

Read Deuteronomy 7. Note why the Israelites were to utterly destroy all the people the Lord God delivered to them.

DAY THREE

Read Deuteronomy 8.

DAY FOUR

Read Deuteronomy 9. Note why God is driving out the nations.

DAY FIVE

Read Deuteronomy 10. Note what the Lord God requires and why.

DAY SIX

Read Deuteronomy 11. Mark the word *curse* and note your insights. Note the two options God has set before the Israelites. Look at the map on page 150 to see where Mount Gerizim and Mount Ebal are located.

DAY SEVEN

Store in your heart: Deuteronomy 6:4,5 or 11:18.
Read and discuss: Deuteronomy 6.

QUESTIONS FOR DISCUSSION OR INDIVIDUAL STUDY

- What would be the danger to the children of Israel once they entered the promised land?

- Do you see the possibility of this same danger in the life of a Christian?

- Why is it a danger?

- How could the children of Israel avoid falling into such a trap? What were God's specific instructions to them in Deuteronomy 6?

- Why didn't God want them to have any other god besides Him? What do you learn about God from this

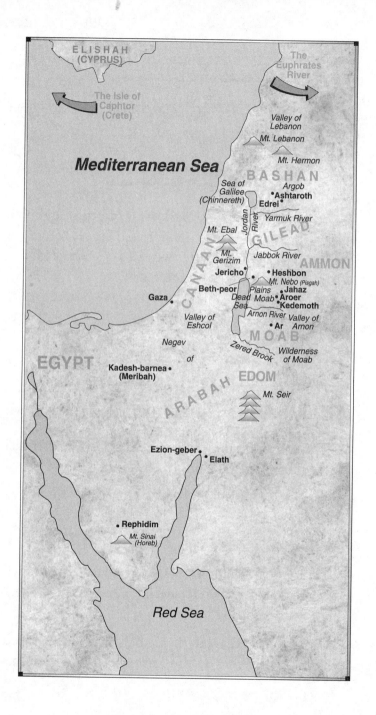

statement? Do you live accordingly, or has God changed? Can He change?

∾ What was Israel's relationship to be to other people? Why?

∾ What do you learn about the Word of God from Deuteronomy 8? What is the illustration God uses and how does it parallel how we should live in respect to the Word of God?

THOUGHT FOR THE WEEK

The things which happened to Israel were to be an example for us, and were written for our instruction, upon whom the end of the ages has come (1 Corinthians 10:11). What examples and lessons there are for us in the book of Deuteronomy! How much do we love our God? How diligent are we about learning His Word so we can keep it before our eyes at all times? What is the most important thing we can teach our children, and how diligent are we in this respect? Are we so busy that we are giving ourselves to that which is temporal and ignoring that which has eternal ramifications?

Are we so concerned about money and earning a living, about gaining more and more, that we have forgotten our God who brought us out of the world, out of bondage to sin?

Beloved, watch yourself lest you forget your God!

WEEK THREE

DAY ONE

In chapters 12 through 16 Moses gives the children of Israel the statutes and the judgments they are to observe. As you read each chapter in this segment of Deuteronomy, record in the margin of each chapter what the people are to do and why. Also note what you learn about God.

Add the following key words and phrase to your bookmark and mark them in your Bible as you work through the remaining chapters of Deuteronomy: *life, death, blessing, you shall purge (remove) the evil.*

Read Deuteronomy 12.

DAY TWO

Read Deuteronomy 13. Watch carefully what is to be done to purge the evil from among the people.

DAY THREE

Read Deuteronomy 14. Mark the word *tithe* and list the instructions regarding the tithe.

DAY FOUR

Read Deuteronomy 15. Mark the word *poor* and list what you learn about dealing with the poor and the kinsman who is sold as a slave.

DAY FIVE

Read Deuteronomy 16. Mark *Passover* and the other feasts mentioned in this chapter. It might be good to consult the chart THE FEASTS OF ISRAEL that is at the end of the Leviticus study.

DAY SIX

Read Deuteronomy 17. Mark the word *king* and all the pronouns which refer to the king. Then list in the margin what you learn about the king.

DAY SEVEN

Store in your heart: Deuteronomy 17:19 and Revelation 5:9,10.

Read and discuss: Deuteronomy 17:14-20.

QUESTIONS FOR DISCUSSION OR INDIVIDUAL STUDY

∾ According to Deuteronomy 17, what two things were the children of Israel to do in order to purge evil from Israel? Why would idolatry be worthy of death? What is so bad about idolatry?

∽ What role were the priests to play? How important was this role? How would a person act presumptuously in this respect?

∽ When a king came to office, what were the things he was to do? List them and discuss their significance. If you have time you might think about the life of King Solomon in respect to these precepts by which the king was to live.

∽ What was the king to do specifically in relationship to the five books of the Bible that you are studying in this book? List every detail and note why it was to be done.

∽ How does all this correlate with Deuteronomy 8:3?

∽ If the king of Israel was to live this way, what does it tell you about how *you* are to live? How are you described in Revelation 5:9,10?

THOUGHT FOR THE WEEK

We are a kingdom—priests unto our God—and we shall someday reign with Him upon this earth. It is an awesome thought. What is even more awesome is that this life is our spiritual boot camp for those days which are to come. We are His slaves, told to occupy until the day comes when Jesus shall reign as King of kings and Lord of lords. The number of cities we reign over will be determined by our stewardship of what He has given us. This is pointed out in Luke 19:11-27.

Are there not valuable and critical lessons to be gleaned from God's instructions in Deuteronomy regarding the man who would be king over Israel?

Beloved, this was written for our example and our instruction, upon whom the end of the age has come. This is the end of the age; Jesus could come at any time. Are you ready?

WEEK FOUR

Continue to follow the general instructions for each chapter as you did last week.

DAY ONE

Read Deuteronomy 18. Mark everything that refers to the enemy, such as *divination, witchcraft,* etc., in a distinctive way.

Mark the word *prophet* and list what you learn regarding prophets.

DAY TWO

Read Deuteronomy 19. Mark *death (die), blood,* and *the avenger of blood.* List what you learn.

DAY THREE

Read Deuteronomy 20. Mark *battle (fight)* and *who is the man.*

DAY FOUR

Read Deuteronomy 21. Note the regulations regarding the shedding of innocent blood, wives, and sons.

DAY FIVE

Read Deuteronomy 22. Note what this chapter teaches regarding immorality.

DAY SIX

Read Deuteronomy 23. This chapter covers a wide variety of regulations. You may want to note the various subjects in the margin of your Bible next to the verse where each subject is introduced.

DAY SEVEN

Store in your heart: Deuteronomy 18:22.
Read and discuss: Deuteronomy 18:9-22.

QUESTIONS FOR DISCUSSION OR INDIVIDUAL STUDY

∞ What are the detestable things listed in Deuteronomy 18 that God does not want the children of Israel to learn or to practice? List them.

∞ Why do you think God deems them detestable?

∞ How do these things compare with today? Are these things available today? What do you think should be our attitude and behavior in the light of what we see in Deuteronomy and in other portions of the Pentateuch?

꙳ There are many people claiming to be prophets today, or allowing others to recognize them as such—prophets in the sense that they are making specific predictions that are not found written out in the Word of God. According to this passage, how would a person be able to spot a false prophet?

꙳ What would be the judgment for a prophet who spoke in the name of God when God hadn't told him to speak?

꙳ What are some of the things mentioned in Deuteronomy that the children of Israel were to do in order to purge evil from among them? List these. As you think about this list, what do you learn about God and His ways?

꙳ What have you learned from your study this week that you need to live in the light of?

THOUGHT FOR THE WEEK

Have you dabbled in any way in the occult? Maybe you have casually read the horoscope section of your newspaper or a magazine. Possibly you have watched the psychics on television and thought, "What harm could it do?" Or maybe out of curiosity you have ordered a book that deals with these subjects. Whether you believe in these "supernatural things" or not, do you think you ought to get involved in these practices?

What do you learn from Deuteronomy about the mind and heart of God on this subject?

And what about all the "prophets" you hear? Do you spend more time listening to them than studying the Word of God? Which is more important? If you don't know what the Word of God says, will you be able to distinguish whether a prophet is speaking from God or not?

How wise you are, Beloved, to study His Word so diligently! When you see your Lord face-to-face, you will be thankful you have disciplined yourself in this way.

WEEK FIVE

❧❧❧❧

DAY ONE

Read Deuteronomy 24. List what you learn regarding the certificate of divorce and the reason for it.

DAY TWO

Read Deuteronomy 25 and 26. Note how Moses brings these various commandments to a conclusion in 26:16-19.

DAY THREE

In Deuteronomy 27–30 Moses lays out the necessity of obedience, laying before the children of Israel the blessings of obedience and the inevitable curses that will come on the disobedient.

Add the following words to your bookmark and mark them in your Bible as you work through the remaining chapters of Deuteronomy: *curse(s)(ed)*, *blessing(s)(blessed)*, *the Lord will*, *nation (nations, enemies, people)*, and *captivity*.

As you read these chapters keep asking the 5 W's and an H. Note who and/or what will be affected by the people's obedience or disobedience. Also note everything that will happen if they obey or disobey.

Read Deuteronomy 27.

DAY FOUR

Read Deuteronomy 28:1-19. Note the areas in which the people would be blessed or cursed.

DAY FIVE

Read Deuteronomy 28:20-68. List everything you learn about the dispersion of the children of Israel because of disobedience. This information will be of great value when you study the history of Israel.

DAY SIX

Read Deuteronomy 29. Mark the word *covenant* and list what you learn.

DAY SEVEN

Store in your heart: Deuteronomy 29:29.

Read and discuss: Deuteronomy 28:20-41,47-68. In your discussion, review the history of Israel. (There is a 12-page synopsis of the history of Israel on pages 2089-2100 in your *NISB*.)

QUESTIONS FOR DISCUSSION OR INDIVIDUAL STUDY

∿ What were the curses that would come on Israel if they didn't obey God and walk in His statutes? What areas of their lives would these curses affect? List them on a board if possible.

∞ Thinking through what you know about the history of Israel, did any of these curses come to pass? When? How? Note them on the board next to each curse that would come.

∞ Are any of them still in effect? If anyone answered yes, ask: How do you know? Why would you say they are still in effect?

∞ What do you learn about God from these curses and Israel's history?

∞ Do you think those who profess to know the Lord Jesus Christ and live in such a way as to violate the precepts of passion, obedience, and behavior laid down in Deuteronomy will escape any sort of judgment by God? Give a biblical reason for your answer.

∞ Did these things come to pass just as the Lord said? What does your answer confirm to you about your God and His Word?

THOUGHT FOR THE WEEK

Many times we are eager to look into the hidden, the unknown. We can even be quick to become caught up with the teacher, preacher, or media personality who shows us things which others have missed—secret things, hidden things, or things which can be understood only by an elite group of Christians.

Whenever this becomes our interest or focus we need to remember that the things God wants us to know are somewhere between Genesis 1:1 and Revelation 22:21.

They are not hidden, but are revealed in the clear teaching of God's Word. Ours is to take the time to totally familiarize ourselves with the content of the Bible. The Word of God is what belongs to you and your sons forever that you might observe all its precepts.

Some may say, "But there's not time—there's so much I have to do just to survive!" If you hear this excuse, suggest to that person that he or she keep a log of the time he spends reading the newspaper, magazines, books, and of the time he spends watching television. And what about the time devoted to interests outside of what it takes to earn a reasonable living (not a luxurious lifestyle, but a reasonable living)?

If you want to live a life pleasing to your God, simply live according to what He has given you in His Book. Then, Beloved, you will hear, "Well done, My good and faithful servant."

Week Six

DAY ONE

Read Deuteronomy 30. Mark the words *heart* and *love*. Note what you learn from marking these words.

DAY TWO

With chapter 31 we come to the final segment of Deuteronomy, which contains Moses' parting words, song, and blessing, as well as the account of his death. Continue to mark the key words listed on your bookmark, and to examine each chapter in the light of the 5 W's and an H.

Read Deuteronomy 31. Mark the phrase *be strong and courageous* and every reference to the book of the law which Moses wrote. In the margin list all that was to be done with the law which Moses wrote.

DAY THREE

Read Deuteronomy 32:1-18. Mark every reference to the Rock. Then list what you learn about the Rock. Give special attention to what you learn about Israel in this chapter. Note what leads to Israel's downfall, and the consequences of it.

Jeshurun in 32:15 is a reference to Israel.

DAY FOUR

Read Deuteronomy 32:19-52. Follow the instructions for yesterday. As you continue to make your list of all you learn regarding the Rock, remember that this was written by a man who was forbidden to enter the promised land after he had led the children of Israel faithfully in the wilderness for 40 years. What does this tell you about Moses and about God?

DAY FIVE

Read Deuteronomy 33. Mark the name of each tribe of Israel and carefully observe what is said about each of them. Underline every occurrence of *they shall* (*they will*) and note what they will do.

DAY SIX

Read Deuteronomy 34. Note what you learn about Moses and about Joshua. Don't forget to record all your insights about Moses.

DAY SEVEN

Store in your heart: Deuteronomy 32:46,47a.

Read and discuss: Deuteronomy 32:1-47. Think about all you learn about God just from this chapter.

QUESTIONS FOR DISCUSSION OR INDIVIDUAL STUDY

∾ What do you learn about God from Moses' song in Deuteronomy 32? List all the things you learn about the character of God and the ways of God.

∾ How should such knowledge affect the way you live? Look at each thing that is listed about God, and then discuss practical ways in which these things should affect your life.

∾ Does it surprise you that Moses would say such things when, after serving God for 80 years, God would not let Moses enter the promised land? What does this tell you about Moses? What does it tell you about God?

∾ How can the lessons you learned in Deuteronomy be of value to you as a child of God living at this time in history?

∾ How did Moses die? Who was to be Moses' successor? Do you think it was a fitting choice? Why? What do you know about Joshua?

THOUGHT FOR THE WEEK

Think about all you have learned about God, His character, and His ways. Then think about Israel. In the book of Deuteronomy God clearly rehearsed the events that brought the Israelites out of the land of Egypt, out of the house of bondage, to the borders of a land He promised to Abraham hundreds of years before. Then God gave them clear instructions on how they were to live when they entered this land flowing with milk and honey. He set before them the statutes and the judgments they were to observe, statutes and judgments that covered every aspect of their lives, statutes and judgments that would set them apart from the other nations. Following these, He spelled out very clearly the blessings that would be theirs if they walked in obedience to these statutes and judgments, as well as the consequences if they disobeyed. Even Moses, their faithful leader, was a testimony to the fact that what God said, He meant—He would not alter the words which went forth from His mouth, even in regard to Moses. Moses pled with God that he might enter the promised land, but God would not relent.

Moses recognized and acknowledged before the whole nation that God's work is perfect, that all His ways are just: "A God of faithfulness and without injustice, righteous and upright is He" (Deuteronomy 32:4).

In His final words through Moses, God also let His people know that although they would not listen, and although the curses would come upon them, He would atone for His land and His people.

This was Israel's hope, and it is yours too, Beloved, so take these words to heart. They are not idle words; they are indeed your life.

Theme of Deuteronomy:

SEGMENT DIVISIONS

		CHAPTER THEMES
		1
		2
		3
		4
		5
		6
		7
		8
		9
		10
		11
		12
		13
		14
		15
		16
		17
		18
		19
		20
		21
		22
		23
		24
		25
		26
		27
		28
		29
		30
		31
		32
		33
		34

Author:

Historical Setting:

Geographical Location:

Purpose:

Key Words:
(including synonyms)

NOTES FOR PERSONAL STUDY

NOTES FOR PERSONAL STUDY

Notes for Personal Study

NOTES FOR PERSONAL STUDY

NOTES FOR PERSONAL STUDY

Harvest House Books
by Kay Arthur

~~~~~

God, Are You There?
God, Help Me Experience More of You
God, How Can I Live?
God, I Need More Comfort
How to Study Your Bible
Israel, My Beloved
Jesus, God's Gift of Hope
Just a Moment with You, God
Lord, Teach Me to Pray in 28 Days
A Marriage Without Regrets
A Marriage Without Regrets Study Guide
Prayers to Bless Your Marriage
Speak to My Heart, God
With an Everlasting Love

Bibles

The New Inductive Study Bible (NASB)

Discover 4 Yourself®
Inductive Bible Studies for Kids

How to Study Your Bible for Kids
Lord, Teach Me to Pray for Kids
God's Amazing Creation (Genesis 1–2)
Digging Up the Past (Genesis 3–11)
Abraham—God's Brave Explorer (Genesis 11–25)
Joseph—God's Superhero (Genesis 37–50)
Wrong Way, Jonah! (Jonah)
Jesus in the Spotlight (John 1–11)
Jesus—Awesome Power, Awesome Love (John 11–16)
Jesus—To Eternity and Beyond! (John 17–21)
Boy, Have I Got Problems! (James)
God, What's Your Name?
Extreme Adventures with God

Books in the
New Inductive Study Series

∾∾∾∾∾

Everybody, Everywhere, Anytime, Anyplace, Any Age...
Can Discover the Truth for Themselves

In today's world with its often confusing and mixed messages, where can you turn to find the answer to the challenges you and your family face? Whose word can you trust? Where can you turn when you need answers—about relationships, your children, your future?

The <u>Updated</u> New Inductive Study Bible

Open *this* study Bible and you will soon discover its uniqueness— unlike any other, this study Bible offers no notes, commentaries, or the opinions of others telling you what the Scripture is saying. It is in fact the only study Bible based entirely on the *inductive* study approach, providing you with instructions and the tools for observing what the text really says, interpreting what it means, and applying its principles to your life.

The only study Bible containing the *inductive study method* taught and endorsed by Kay Arthur and Precept Ministries.

• A new *smaller* size makes it easier to carry • individualized instructions for studying *every* book • guides for color marking keywords and themes • *Updated* NASB text • *improved* in-text maps and charts • 24 pages of full-color charts, historical timelines, & maps • self-discovery in its truest form

One Message, The Bible.
One Method, Inductive.

A SIMPLE, PROVEN APPROACH TO LETTING GOD'S WORD CHANGE YOUR LIFE...FOREVER

HARVEST HOUSE™
PUBLISHERS
EUGENE, OREGON

DIGGING DEEPER

ର୍ଗେର୍ଗେ

Books in the New Inductive Study Series are survey courses. If you want to do a more in-depth study of a particular book of the Bible, we suggest that you do a Precept Upon Precept Bible Study Course on that book. The Precept studies require approximately five hours of personal study a week. You may obtain more information on these powerful courses by contacting Precept Ministries International at 800-763-8280, visiting our website at www.precept.org, or filling out and mailing the response card in the back of this book.

If you desire to expand and sharpen your skills, you would really benefit by attending a Precept Ministries Institute of Training. The Institutes are conducted throughout the United States, Canada, and in a number of other countries. Class lengths vary from one to five days, depending on the course you are interested in. For more information on the Precept Ministries Institute of Training, call Precept Ministries.

YES, I WANT TO GROW SPIRITUALLY.
TELL ME MORE ABOUT

PRECEPT MINISTRIES INTERNATIONAL

Name _____

Address _____

City_____

State_____ Postal Code _____

Country_____

Daytime phone (___)_____

Email address _____

Fax (___)_____

Evening phone (___)_____

PLEASE SEND ME INFO ON:

❑ Learning how to study the Bible

❑ Bible study material

❑ Radio Programs

❑ TV Programs

❑ Israel Bible Study Tour

❑ Paul's Epistles Study Tour to Greece

❑ Men's Conferences

❑ Women's Conferences

❑ Teen Conferences

❑ Couples' Conferences

❑ Other_____

❑ I want to partner with Precept Ministries

   ENCLOSED IS MY DONATION FOR $_____

P.O. Box 182218 • Chattanooga, TN 37422-7218
(800) 763-8280 • (423) 892-6814 • Radio/TV (800) 763-1990
Fax: (423) 894-2449 • www.precept.org • Email: info@precept.org